Images of Protestantism in America

Robert L. Ferm

FORTRESS PRESS • MINNEAPOLIS

To Sonja

PIETY, PURITY, PLENTY
Images of Protestantism in America

Cover and interior design: Ned Skubic

Library of Congress Cataloging-in-Publication Data

Ferm, Robert L.
    Piety, purity, plenty : images of Protestantism in America /
Robert L. Ferm.
        p.   cm.
    Includes bibliographical references and index.
    ISBN 0-8006-2454-8 (alk. paper)
    1. Protestant churches—United States.   2. United States—
Religion—1960–   I. Title.
BR526.F47   1991
280'.4'0973—dc20   90-21620
                                                                          CIP

Manufactured in the U.S.A.   AF 1-2454
95   94   93   92   91   1   2   3   4   5   6   7   8   9   10

CONTENTS

Preface

This volume is addressed to the "cultured despisers" and disenchanted lovers of the Christian church.
While the days of Christians battling the "infidel" are
over, except among the few lingering defenders of the
faith, many people stand on the periphery. And while
mainline Protestantism is no longer troubled by heresy,
many people are no longer engaged by their religious
heritage. They are on the outside, looking in, seeking
to understand why they have become disenchanted or
even covert or overt cultured despisers. Others who once
struggled to understand what has happened in the
churches now have lapsed into a quiescent acceptance
that what once mattered no longer does.

For these people I seek to articulate the various images of Protestantism that have, for good or ill, determined its identity in the United States. Therein, I believe,
lie clues to the disenchantment and alienation that many
experience.

So in this work I describe the way in which many
have viewed the Christian faith, particularly Protestantism, in America, and I indicate some of the historical
sources for those "images." Yet this is not a historical
essay alone but also a theological affirmation. A historian
can describe, however incompletely, the dominant emphases of a period; a theologian asks very different
questions. Yet the division of labor is not clear-cut. A
historian is also an interpreter of history for his or

her contemporaries, and a theologian, particularly a Christian theologian, also draws deeply from historical sources. As a participant in and observer of American religious life, I have been continually impressed by how much we as Americans apparently hold religiously dear and yet how little we understand about what we believe. Defensively I ask, why is this so? Historically I ask, how did this come about? Theologically I ask, what is the nature of this Christian faith? Those are the questions this volume briefly addresses.

My focus is on so-called mainline Protestantism, an awkward but frequently used term. *Mainline* means basically the familiar, white, middle-of-the-road denominational traditions that trace their origin to the Reformation of the sixteenth century and whose traditional theological affirmations are tied to that formative period. Ecclesiastically it covers the spectrum from Episcopalian to Baptist; theologically it includes the range from self-described "evangelicals" to liberals. It lacks precise definition, but by and large it is self-conscious enough to regard some as fringe groups and some theological positions as marginally Protestant. Mainline Protestants are comfortable with the simple adjective *Protestant* or *Christian,* but they are not necessarily conscious of the historical particularity of the ecclesiastical or theological tradition to which they belong.

Historians may write of the last decades of this century as a time of corrective rather than constructive theology. The dominant theological voices of our time seek to right wrongs, to interpret the Christian faith primarily in terms of its response to wider social and cultural change. That is as it should be. Yet the theological options presented frequently divide or require sophisticated intellectual gymnastics to discover how they could possibly relate to the church. Until World War II most theology was written by those who had been or still were pastors. Times have changed, and it is my conviction that in the process something has also been lost. This book has grown out of that concern to raise again fundamental questions about Christianity's historical and contemporary identity.

I express my gratitude to those colleagues, unnamed but known, who have been steadfast in my wayward journey and to the students from whom I have learned, most particularly that unique group in the Class of 1979 at Middlebury College.

—Robert L. Ferm

Introduction

A recent article in *Time* magazine, "Those Mainline Blues," described the troubles besetting "America's Old Guard Protestant Churches."[1] Its authors painted a bleak picture. Since 1965 five major denominations—United Church of Christ, Presbyterian, Episcopalian, Methodist, and Disciples of Christ—have lost among them 5.2 million members during a period when the nation's population grew by 47 million people. One commentator stated, "Not only are the traditional denominations failing to get their message across; they are increasingly unsure just what that message is." It also may be that the message they are sending no longer has any meaning.

Mainline Protestantism has shaped the beliefs of many Americans. A recent study has indicated that, among Western nations, the United States has the highest percentage of citizens claiming membership in a church or religious group, surpassing Northern Ireland and far surpassing Denmark, France, Italy, West Germany, or Great Britain. In fact, 43 percent of Americans claim that they attend religious services once a week, comparable in numbers to such traditionally religious nations as the two Irelands and Spain. And Americans apparently are far more religiously active than people in Denmark (3 percent), France (12 percent), or Great Britain (14 percent). Fully 95 percent of Americans say they believe in God (only 2 percent say no), while in Sweden, for example, 52 percent say yes and 35 percent say no.

Again, 84 percent of Americans believe in heaven, while only 17 percent in Denmark and 41 percent in Italy claim to do so. The same poll asks questions about the Ten Commandments: does each one apply fully today, or only to a limited extent, or not at all? United States citizens came out once again either at the top or next to the top of the respondents who said each commandment applied fully.[2] Though the questions oversimplify religious belief and cannot gauge its tenacity, depth, or thoughtfulness, the poll at least indicates a consistency in attitude on the part of those being questioned.

A subtler picture of American religious belief emerged from an earlier survey, designed to measure belief patterns within particular mainline Protestant denominations. Its directors, Charles Glock and Rodney Stark, suggested that significant differences in beliefs among mainline Protestant denominations are still present, despite the general religiousness of Americans that most surveys have noted. Their study indicated that theological disagreements are not just "between Christians and secular society, although this is certainly true as well, but exist substantially *within* the formal boundaries of the Christian churches."[3] This point has often not been as emphasized as it should be. The theological heritage of some denominations has continued to be stressed, even though the meaning of the words may have subtly changed over the course of years.

For example, concerning belief in God, Glock and Stark asked, "Which of the following statements come closest to what you believe about God?" The first possible response was, "I know God really exists and I have no doubts about it." (The other five statements were less affirmative and ended with, "I don't believe in God.") Among respondents, the Southern Baptists and sectarian groups ranked highest at 99 percent and 96 percent respectively, followed by Missouri Synod Lutherans and Catholics at 81 percent, Episcopalians at 63 percent, and Congregationalists at 41 percent.

2

To characterize religious belief about Jesus, Glock and Stark asked, "Which of the following statements comes closest to what you believe about Jesus?" One option was, "Jesus is the Divine Son of God and I have no doubts about it." Responding yes were 99 percent of Southern Baptists, 97 percent of sectarian groups, 93 percent of Missouri Synod Lutherans, 72 percent of Presbyterians, 59 percent of Episcopalians, 54 percent of Methodists, and 40 percent of Congregationalists. Another traditional doctrine, "Jesus was born of a virgin," was affirmed by those who responded, "completely true." They included Southern Baptists, 99 percent; sectarian groups, 96 percent; Missouri Synod Lutherans, 93 percent; Presbyterians, 57 percent; Episcopalians, 39 percent; and Congregationalists, 21 percent.

On the subject of sin, pollsters asked whether respondents would affirm the statement, "Man cannot help doing evil" (note the wording "*doing* evil"). Affirmative responses came from Missouri Synod Lutherans, 63 percent; Southern Baptists, 62 percent; sectarian groups, 37 percent; Episcopalians, 30 percent; Catholics, 22 percent; and Congregationalists, 21 percent. "A child is born into the world already guilty of sin." The percent who affirmed the statement as completely true included Missouri Synod Lutherans, 86 percent; Catholics, 68 percent; sectarian groups, 47 percent; Southern Baptists, 43 percent; Presbyterians, 21 percent; Episcopalians, 18 percent; Methodists, 7 percent; and Congregationalists, 2 percent.

Glock and Stark's study confirms that some denominational traditions continue to have a greater emphasis on particular theological affirmations. The Missouri Synod Lutherans, for example, continue to stress a high Christology and a strong sense of sin, which have been part of their confessional Lutheran heritage. The Episcopalians, who have not emphasized doctrinal issues but rather liturgical ones, have a greater degree of flexibility. Congregationalists are consistently the loosest in their theological affirmations. Some theological self-consciousness remains in some denominations.

Although Americans exhibit a general religiosity and make Christian language their own, there is no indication that they have given much thought to the substance of their beliefs, except to some degree in the most confessionally oriented traditions. That is, Americans are not theologically literate or articulate. During the course of our history there has emerged an ever-increasing gulf between the laity and the theologians. This was not the case in seventeenth- or eighteenth-century New England, but the gap increased during the course of the nineteenth century and probably is wider today than ever before. The distancing of Americans from their theological roots is happening despite evidence that church membership among Americans reached its high point in the 1950s and the decline since then has been only modest.

Until recent years most theological debates revolved around "liberal" and "fundamentalist" concerns. No longer are those issues the dominant ones. By and large lay people today would be puzzled and perplexed if they participated in or even read the annual program of the American Academy of Religion, even more specifically those sections that deal with Christian theology. The variety of academic theological options increases annually, and new schools of thought and new disciples seem to proliferate freely. Particularly in the past two decades, the work of theologians seems to be shaped much more by the religious import of so-called secular concerns—economic and political liberation, the black experience, feminism, process philosophy, and literary criticism. Their work is important and vital, but it does not evidently or compellingly address the broader dilution of Christians' religious identity today in the way we propose.[4]

My task is to deal with more subtle factors than statistics or a survey of the themes in contemporary theology, namely to describe the images that many in

4

the United States have of Protestantism. Images do not necessarily duplicate reality; they are shaped by our individual and collective histories. The Christian faith has developed over the centuries by responding to intellectual and social currents, of which theologians and church people have been a part and which in turn shaped their understanding. That simple truism is sometimes forgotten. Doctrine was not formulated in a vacuum. The biblical writers were not removed from their particular context when they attempted to articulate the good news. Martin Luther and John Calvin were participants in the ferment of the sixteenth century. Black theology and feminist theology are formulated explicitly in response to fundamental changes taking place in our society.

There may or may not be an "American" Protestantism, but there are factors that have given a distinctive character to our understanding of Protestantism in America and, therefore, created the images I describe. As a descriptive judgment, I note that these images are theologically distinct from their roots in the major themes of the sixteenth-century Protestant Reformation. As a normative judgment, I argue that much that is distinctive about the Christian faith has been lost in the development of Protestantism in America. I do not suggest that sixteenth-century views can be transplanted without change into our period in history. I do suggest that if the thrust of the concerns in regard to human nature that shaped much of Western theological history and particularly the Protestant reformers, Martin Luther and John Calvin, is forgotten, then we do have a different and diluted Christian faith. Nor do I wish to imply that the words of a Luther or a Calvin, or their world views, are to be seen as infallible texts to replace an "infallible" Scripture. Rather, I believe that the anthropological issue with which they wrestled is the one that should be at the forefront of our concern today. In its place we have what might be called the "American heresy" of viewing the Christian as a morally pious, uncritical purist who

5

reveres the plethora of religious options confronting us and therefore becomes almost lukewarmly tolerant of anything that seems to be ambiguously Christian.

The images or themes of piety, purity, and plenty describe the ways in which the Christian faith is often understood by many. Chapter 1 considers an example of each of these. By "plenty" is meant the variety of Christian options that have developed in American history. Though there were different traditions active in our history before the American Revolution, frequently these groups were confronted by established churches. Gradually during the course of the nineteenth century and especially after ratification of the Fourteenth Amendment (1868), which made the First Amendment applicable to the states, the prohibition of established churches became the law of the land. Many new immigrant denominations sought to nurture their traditions without state interference, and many indigenous American denominations began to prosper. Visitors to the new United States from Europe in the nineteenth century were struck by this experiment in what is usually called church–state relations but more properly should be seen as a religion–state issue. With certain exceptions (for example, the practice of polygamy in the Church of Jesus Christ of the Latter-Day Saints), these groups were adapting to the American scene. Many of the foreign travelers were struck by the attention given to religious, namely Christian, matters. This "Christian" element in the history of nineteenth-century America has been noted by many and is an essential ingredient in our self-understanding. In the process of the development of the image of plenty, the lines of demarcation among groups became blurred but not completely erased.

Included in this chapter, as an illustration of the image of purity, is an imaginary conversation with Robert Ingersoll, a self-professed infidel who viewed Christianity as benighted and Christians as holding views that no enlightened individual could possibly affirm. He pokes fun, caricatures Christian faith, and makes it seem as nonsensical as he possibly can. Others have done the same, and the image they presuppose is not simply a relic of a bygone age. In addition, the image of piety is represented by the moral evangelist, with the example of Jerry Falwell, who defines Christianity in specific moral terms and with the appropriate fervor of a revivalist. The succeeding chapters outline some of the historical reasons for these images of piety, purity, and plenty.

Chapter 2 is concerned with the theme or image that became dominant in many denominations during the nineteenth century—piety—namely, understanding Christian faith not in terms of its theological heritage but rather in terms of morality. Subtly but surely, in Christian terms, the presupposition concerning human nature became that "one can if one will" and "the good will be known by their fruits." If the human being can know and do the will of God, then it is possible to judge with some reliable yardstick who is and who is not a Christian. The Christian is known by one's behavior and, frequently, one's heartfelt experience. That image remains with us.

Chapter 3 suggests that the image of purity depicts the Christian faith in propositional terms, that certain tenets are necessarily "Christian." This understanding is present not only within conservative theological circles but also in the minds of many who claim the label *Christian* but have not given the faith much thought. It remains with us in large part because we have not yet come to grips with the effects of the Enlightenment. Many today remain convinced that the faith was once and for all delivered to the saints.

Chapter 4 briefly considers the formation and some of the effects of the First Amendment in the modern period. I have chosen to use the image of plenty, meaning the variety or pluralism of Christian alternatives that are present in our nation and the importance that generalized religious themes still have. Recent decisions of the Supreme Court in interpreting the First Amendment's clauses concerning the establishment and free exercise of religion reflect some of the legal difficulties of the relation of "religion" and government. These two clauses have made the so-called wall of separation between church and state much more ambiguous than many might wish. The image of plenty is also an ingredient in the elusive "civil religion" that appears in political pronouncements and creates the impression that it is somehow "un-American" to challenge the deeply held convictions of some in deference to the frequently too-easy god of toleration.

The dominance of and tensions among these three images have shaped American religious life. It is their inadequacy that accounts for the dilution of Christian identity today. In chapter 5, I outline another way to understand the themes of the Christian faith in contemporary terms and to challenge the presuppositions of the dominant images that have been described. This is a beginning and not an end. I suggest that we must take seriously the roots of the Protestant theological tradition in order to claim the label at all. Much of what exists today under the rubric *Protestant* is a distortion of the assumption that fundamentally the Christian faith is a distinctive understanding of human nature and human redemption. We have become leery of the words *sin* and *redemption,* in large part because of the moralistic, pietistic, and literalistic meaning those words convey. Chapter 5 envisions a constructive alternative.

$\mathcal{C}$HAPTER 1
Images of Protestantism in America

To define the word *Christian* is not as easy as it may seem. The obvious proposals—a follower of Jesus Christ, a member of a Christian church—are not very informative or theologically meaningful. To say that a Christian is one who accepts Jesus Christ as Lord and Savior and has had a "born again" experience adds something to the definition. But it also raises additional questions: What is meant by "savior"? What does it mean to be "born again"?

Despite the difficulty of precise definition, the word *Christian* is part of our common vocabulary, and we frequently employ the term in quite different ways and therefore talk on quite different levels. We have different images of what a Christian is, and those images are shaped by our histories and experiences. This chapter attempts to outline some of those images, indicating how other people have viewed the Christian faith and how their images may well have shaped our own.

The Foreign Traveler: The Image of Plenty

For many on the European continent and in England, America was a land of bewildering character. During the late eighteenth and throughout the nineteenth centuries, numerous men and women, as individuals and in groups, toured the developing New World. Some of them came with intense prejudices, which they wished to (and frequently did) corroborate. Others entered to compare customs and institutions of the new country with their homeland. Still others were intrigued enough to want to know if this was where they wished to spend their lives. The visitors came to observe theatrical life, to learn about treatment of blacks and the practice of slavery, to compare legislative processes with those of their homeland, to investigate sites of geologic interest, and for many other personal reasons. Travelers are prone to make quick judgments and comparisons. Their numerous accounts are of uneven quality. Some writers, such as Francis Grund, C. W. Janson, Alexander Mackay, and Alexis de Tocqueville, offered perceptive analyses. Others, such as Frances Trollope or Frederick Marryat, were highly prejudiced and superficial, although not without entertaining qualities.

Every traveler to America in the nineteenth century who had some comment to make about the religious character of the land was struck by the principle of voluntarism, that each church was to be dependent on its own resources and not those of government. No trait seemed so distinctive as this pluralism, this image of plenty. Although certainly not all came to observe American religious life, those who had comments to make were preoccupied by the experiment in church–state relations. Some commentators said that before they had come they had been exceedingly skeptical of the effects of the constitutional guarantee of freedom of worship. This principle, they argued, would lead to religious anarchy and a gradual dissipation of religious conviction among the American people. Because these visitors came from lands where the close relation of church and state was assumed, they purposely sought to examine how the system worked in practice. The principle of voluntarism, then, was the most frequently observed trait

of American religious life. This principle meant, in ecclesiastical terms, that the church was a voluntary association, independent of civil control; the only arm of
power in religious affairs was persuasion, not coercion.
Out of this root grew the practices that attracted the
attention of the travelers.

The implications of Jefferson's "Act for Establishing
Religious Freedom," which was presented to the Virginia legislature in 1779, made foreign observers wary
of the burgeoning structure of American religious
groups. A key passage in that act read:

> Be it therefore enacted by the General Assembly.
> That no man shall be compelled to frequent or
> support any religious worship, place or ministry
> whatsoever, nor shall be enforced, restrained,
> molested, or burthened in his body or goods,
> nor shall otherwise suffer on account of his reli-
> gious opinions or belief; but that all men shall be
> free to profess, and by argument to maintain,
> their opinions in matters of religion, and that the
> same shall in nowise diminish, enlarge, or affect
> their civil capacities.[1]

This meant that no restrictions could be placed on the
proliferation of sects. Under the principle of voluntarism, any form of religious expression must be granted
the protection of the state. Although the Dunker (German Baptist Brethren) was regarded as a deviation from
an elusive norm, he or she was no less American than
the Congregationalist. The Frenchman J. Hector St. John
de Crevecoeur, who settled in America in the late eighteenth century, remarked: " 'Tis incredible to what a
pitch this indulgence is carried; and 'tis equally surprising
how beneficial it has proved. . . . Here not only every
community, but every individual worships God as he
thinks most agreeable to him. Each individual is even
allowed, not by virtue of any laws, but by the liberal

11

spirit of the government, to differ from and controvert any of the religious opinions which are here received."[2]

The underlying assumption that America was a Christian nation prevailed; freedom of religious expression was not to be seen as a threat to this foundation of the American way. In 1880 James Bryce remarked that Americans "deem the general acceptance of Christianity to be one of the main successes of their national prosperity, and their nation a special object of the Divine favour." Brycc also pointed to the developing views of the state held by Americans, which allowed the principle of voluntarism to be effective and to thrive.

> The state is not to them [Americans], as to Germans or Dutchmen, and even to some English thinkers, an ideal moral power, charged with the duty of forming the characters and guiding the lines of its subjects. It is more like a commercial company, or perhaps a huge municipality created for the management of certain business in which all who reside within its bounds are interested, levying contributions and expending them in this business of common interest, but for the most part leaving the shareholders or burgesses to themselves. That an organization of this kind should trouble itself, otherwise than as matter of policy, with the opinions or conduct of its members, would be as unnatural as for a railway company to inquire how many of the shareholders were Wesleyans or total abstainers. Accordingly it never occurs to the average American that there is any reason why state churches should exist, and he stands amazed at the warmth of European feeling on the matter. . . . So far from thinking their commonweal the godless, [the American] . . . conceives that the religious character of a government consists in nothing but the religious

belief of the individual citizens, and the
conformity of their conduct to that belief.[3]

This view of the state and the related principle of voluntarism served as the basis out of which grew the distinctive characteristics of American religious life.

For survival the church had to adopt means compatible with the pattern of church–state relations. With the principle of voluntarism grew competition for church members, or perhaps more accurately, different options for the saving of souls. As Francis Grund remarked in 1837: "The American ministers are continually striving to make proselytes, and, being usually paid in proportion to the number of their respective congregations. . . . The principle of paying most 'where most work is done,' or where it is done best, which is daily producing miracles in the United States, is even applicable to the clergy, and is productive of more good to mankind than could be produced with twice the funds in any country in Europe."[4] The Americans, observed Grund, enjoy a threefold advantage: more preachers, more active preachers, and "cheaper" preachers than can be found anywhere else. Voluntarism produced a spirit of energetic activity on the part of the clergy.

Sermons, many observed, also seemed to be shaped by the unique structure of American church life. Less attention was given to doctrinal discourses, which tended to alienate a congregation. More attention was given to sermons of practical tone. John Leng, publisher of the *Dundee Advisor,* contrasted English and American preaching.

> The difference is in their being less clerical in tone and manner and more human. There are many styles of preachers, but all are less professional—less addicted to the use of stereotyped phrases—more direct, homely, and practical than with us. They do not show so much of the scaffolding in the structure of their discourses, by

announcing a number of heads, sub-heads, last-
ly's, finally's and in conclusions. They also seem
to model their sermons more after the style of
Christ's own sermons, instead of following, as
ours commonly do, the epistolary style of St.
Paul. They deal largely in anecdote and illustration.[5]

Commentators who make this type of assessment
usually do so with a tone of criticism of their native
preachers. Not all, however, were positive in their remarks concerning the effects of the voluntaristic principle. The English Presbyterian parson George Lewis
was highly critical of the excesses and divisiveness that
the American church had developed. He saw even the
clergy becoming captives of competition. "There is no
denying that the ministers of religion, in the present
Church system of America, can feel little of real independence in their pecuniary concerns, and must in no
small degree be . . . secularized by their mode of worldly
support." The concern for growth and results brought
diminished emphasis on consideration of substantive
questions of the faith. Lewis berated the American
churches for their lack of interest in educating the young
in Scripture and the "peculiar doctrines of the Protestant
faith." He, unlike most, anticipated that the separation
of church and state would make sharper the separation
of church and world, and, he remarked, "in this I am
not disappointed."[6]

The revivalistic spirit of American religious life in
the nineteenth century was seen as a natural outgrowth
of the voluntaristic principle. If there was no state support of a particular religious form and if the only force
tolerated for the promulgation of the gospel and the
outreach of the church was persuasion, then techniques
for evangelism needed to be developed. These "measures," many observers were surprised to find, perme-
ated all the churches and corresponded to no observable
social divisions.

Social jealousies connected with religions scarcely exist in America. . . . There is a rivalry between the leading denominations to extend their bounds, to erect and fill new churches, to raise great sums for church purposes. . . . It may appear a foolish rivalry but it is not unfriendly, and does not provoke bad blood, because the state stands neutral, and all churches have a free field.[7]

There are, Charles Lyell observed, "no sects to which it is *ungenteel* to belong, no consciences sorely tempted by ambitions to conform to a more fashionable creed."[8]

John Leng, in relating his visit to a rural Baptist church, found much in American church life that was distasteful in comparison with that of his Scottish parish. He reported the words of one minister.

I am a minister of the gospel, one of God's ministers, not one of man's ministers. Thank God I was never within the walls of a College. I not only thank God that I was never within the walls of a College, but I never study my sermons, but trust to God that he will supply all my wants. I do not even chuse my text. I come to the pulpit, trusting to God both for my text and what I am to say upon it. I do not even know this morning on what I am to speak, but I open the Bible thus, and have fallen on this text, "am fearfully and wonderfully made!" Yes, brethren, I have often been accused of being fearfully and wonderfully *mad* when I preach the gospel in these parts.[9]

It is understandable why such sentiments would affect the sensitivities of this Scottish Presbyterian.

Grund, among others, also noted a common moral ethos as another feature of American religious life, a

15

"Christian" character that had pervaded the culture and that was shaped by Enlightenment interests. In relation to governmental activity, he remarked that "religious habits" shaped the Americans' entire view of governmental action; these habits could not be changed without affecting the very essence of their government.

> Religion has been the basis of the most important American settlements; religion kept their little community together—religion assisted them in their revolutionary struggle; it was religion to which they appealed in defending their rights, and it was religion, in fine, which taught them to prize their liberties. It is with the solemnities of religion that the declaration of independence is yet annually read to the people from the pulpit, or that Americans celebrate the anniversaries of the most important events in their history. It is to religion they have recourse whenever they wish to impress the popular feeling with anything relative to their country; and it is religion which assists them in all their national undertakings. The Americans look upon religion as a promoter of civil and political liberty; and have, therefore, transferred to it a large portion of the affection which they cherish for the institutions of their country. In other countries, where religion has become the instrument of oppression, it has been the policy of the liberal party to *diminish* its influence; but in America its promotion is essential to the constitution.[10]

It is worth noting that recent discussions concerning civil religion reflect a similar theme.[11]

Grund, as well as others, recognized some theological differences among the various religious traditions yet most observers also recognized some indefinite lines around which respectable people were to conduct or orient their lives. The moral person is a religious person, and the denial of any religious item of substance brought into question one's moral character; a tarnished moral character was a threat to the stability of the American experiment. Again, Grund:

> The deference which the Americans pay to morality is scarcely inferior to their regard for religion, and is, in part, based on the latter. The least solecism in the moral conduct of a man is attributed to his want of religion, and is visited upon him as such. It is not the offence itself, but the outrage on society, which is punished. They see in a breach of morals a direct violation of religion; and in this, an attempt to subvert the political institutions of the country. These sentiments are all powerful in checking the appearance of vice, even if they are not always sufficient to preclude its existence.
>
> With Argus-eyes does public opinion watch over the words and actions of individuals, and, whatever may be their private sins, enforces at least a tribute to morality in public. . . . The whole people of the United States [are] re-empanneled as a permanent jury to pronounce their verdict of "guilty" or "not guilty" on the conduct and actions of men, from the President down to the laborers; and there is no appeal from their decision.[12]

The moral ethos noted by these travelers had more than Jeffersonian root and character. American mainline Protestantism was an issue from the Enlightenment and this offspring was dressed in evangelistic clothes. The principle of voluntarism bred sectarianism, and sectarianism fed on revivalism.

Although mainline American Protestant religious life until the turn of the nineteenth century preserved its

Calvinistic heritage in theology and ecclesiology, beginning in the nineteenth century it became shaped by Pietism. Those ecclesiastical traditions that were to have the most influence were products of pietistic fervor, seen especially in the Methodists and Baptists. Since the survival of the church depended on solicitation and energetic enthusiasm, it was natural to expect that the more active the parsons and parishioners, the more certain became their "success."

In theology the mood of the nineteenth century was that of Calvinism, with its heart dampened (or enlivened) by the Enlightenment and Pietism. The fervent soul became one who offered evidence of his or her regenerate condition to the world, not, as the Puritan most properly did, to his or her own congregation. The zeal, however, by which clergymen sought to save souls came to have its effect on the larger religious scene and even in churches that otherwise might have been more decorous.

In 1922 G. K. Chesterton commented on what he saw as a basic trait of American culture, one that had its root in the early nineteenth century.

> If I were asked for a single symbolic figure
> summing up the whole of what seems eccentric
> and interesting but American to an Englishman,
> I should be satisfied to select that one lady who
> complained of Mrs. Asquith's lecture and
> wanted her money back. I do not mean that she
> was typically American in complaining; far from
> it. I, for one, have a great and guilty knowledge
> of all that amiable American audiences will
> endure without complaint. I do not mean that
> she was typically American in wanting her
> money; quite the contrary. That sort of American spends money rather than hoards it; and
> when we convict them of vulgarity we acquit
> them of avarice. Where she was typically American, summing up a truth individual and
> indescribable in any other way, is that she used

18

the words: "I've risen from a sick-bed to come and hear her, and I want my money back." [The Englishman] cannot understand a person being proud of serious sacrifices for what is not a serious thing. He does not like to admit that a little thing can excite him; that he can lose his breath in running, or lose his balance in reaching, after something that might be called silly. Now that is where the American is fundamentally different. To him the enthusiasm itself is meritorious. To him the excitement itself is dignified. . . . His ideal is not to be a lock that only a worthy key can open, but a "live wire" that anything can touch or anybody can use. [Americans] would fast or bleed to win a race of paper boats on a pond. They would rise from a sick-bed to listen to Mrs. Asquith.[13]

Too much can be made out of Chesterton's comment, but most travelers were impressed by the zeal and enthusiasm of the people—not only in religion but in all aspects of culture. Few made any comments about intellectual currents or the theological work being done, but few could resist noting the fervor of American life, especially in religious matters. What they saw outdid anything they had encountered before.

The image of plenty as seen by the foreign traveler was evident in the variety of religious groups that grew in nineteenth-century America. They were fed by the new measures of revivalism, which created an atmosphere in which fervor rather than thought was paramount, a fervor that tied together moral behavior and common-denominator religious belief.

The Infidel: The Image of Purity

The enthusiastic infidel is no more. Even the label recalls to our minds a past era of American life. Yet it was not many years ago that Mark Twain, H. L. Mencken, and Robert Ingersoll made clergy angry and ready to do battle to save the faith. Today it might be more appropriate to suggest that the "heirs of heresy" exist within the churches, not without, and a significant part of the critique of Christianity that was made by the infidel is now shared by many of the disenchanted lovers of the church. Christian faith, however, retains the image of being pure, of having tenets that are written in stone and certain items of faith that must be believed. Such characterization of the Christian faith is the image of purity.

To illustrate this image I have devised the following imaginary interview with Robert Ingersoll (1833–99), a self-proclaimed infidel. For him, *infidel* was a term of honor, not of disapprobation. He insisted that we have suffered too long under the cloud of religion and that the time was ripe for people of courage to arise and throw off the shackles of the past. His grandfather had been a member of the Revolutionary army; his father, John Ingersoll, an itinerant pastor. His mother, Mary Livingston, was the daughter of a judge in New York State and the granddaughter of John Livingston, who had migrated to America with the Scotch-Irish Presbyterians during the late eighteenth century.

Ingersoll was well versed in the religious climate of the latter half of the nineteenth century in America. His father, a graduate of Middlebury College, studied theology with a parson in New Haven, Vermont, before being ordained a Congregational minister. During the early years of Robert Ingersoll's life, the family moved from parish to parish across the eastern half of the United States: from Pittsford, Vermont, through several small villages in upper New York State to New York City, then to Wisconsin, Pennsylvania, Illinois, and Ohio. John Ingersoll was a friend and understudy of the famed revivalist Charles Grandison Finney. His son had been prepared to follow his father's vocation. Robert Ingersoll was competent in Hebrew, Greek, and Latin. He had read widely in the patristic writers, Augustine, John Calvin, and Jonathan Edwards. He memorized the Shorter Catechism and even in later years could recite it accurately. From his father's instruction and periods of study in Baptist and Congregationalist preparatory schools, he became quite familiar with biblical writings.

Ingersoll's career was varied. For a time he taught school in Illinois, Ohio, and Tennessee; later he began the study of law, which was to be his main vocation. In 1855 he settled in Peoria, Illinois, where he was active in pre-Civil War political debates, supporting at first Stephen Douglas and later Abraham Lincoln. After service as a colonel in the Union army, he returned to Peoria and began to read with great interest the works of Thomas Paine, August Comte, and Voltaire—authors unknown to him in his youth. In 1877 he moved to Washington, D.C. In the years that followed he toured the country, gaining fame as a controversial and stimulating platform orator.

This friend of presidents, literary figures, and leaders in the business world was an outspoken "freethinker." His collected works now fill twelve volumes; thousands heard him speak, thousands applauded, thousands criticized. In the interview that follows he presents a part of his case against Christianity. The questions are mine; the words are his.

Q. You take great pride in being called an infidel. Why?

A. "Well, let us see. In the first place, what is an 'infidel'? He is simply a man in advance of his time. He is an intellectual pioneer. . . . All advance has been made by 'infidels,' by 'heretics,' by skeptics, by doubters— that is to say by thoughtful men. . . . The 'heretic' is not true to falsehood. Orthodoxy is. He who stands faithfully by a mistake is 'orthodox.' He who, discovering that it is a mistake, has the courage to say so, is an 'infidel.' "[14]

Q. You have said much in criticism of the Bible and why an infidel finds it impossible to take it seriously. Why?

A. "One of the foundation stones of our faith is the Old Testament. . . . According to the Bible, Adam was certainly the first man, and in his case the epoch theory [of creation] cannot change the account. The Bible gives the age at which Adam died, and gives the generations to the flood—then to Abraham and so on, and shows that from the creation of Adam to the birth of Christ it was about four thousand and four years.

"According to the sacred Scriptures man has been on this earth five thousand eight hundred and ninety-nine years *and* no more.

"According to the Bible the first man was created four thousand and four years before Christ.

"According to the same Bible there was a flood some fifteen or sixteen hundred years after Adam was created that destroyed the entire human race with the exception of eight persons, and according to the Bible the Egyptians descended from one of the sons of Noah.

"According to that book the sun was made after the earth was created.

"The New Testament vouches for the truth, the inspiration, of the Old, and if the Old is false, the New cannot be true" (4:239–49).

Q. You apparently feel that the Bible is the creation of simple-minded and deluded men.

A. "All that is necessary, as it seems to me, to convince any reasonable person that the Bible is simply and purely of human invention—of barbarian invention—is to read it. Read it as you would any other book; think of it as you would of any other; get the bandage of reverence from your eyes; drive from your heart the phantom of fear; push from the throne of your brains the cowled form of superstition—then read the Holy Bible, and you will be amazed that you ever, for one moment, supposed a being of infinite wisdom, goodness and purity, to be the author of such ignorance and of such atrocity" (1:17).

Q. I assume that you would make no distinctions between the Old and New Testaments.

A. "In the New Testament, death is not the end, but the beginning of punishment that has no end. In the New Testament the malice of God is infinite and the hunger of his revenge eternal. . . . God so loved the world that he made up his mind to damn a large majority of the human race" (4:207, 24).

Q. What about the training of Protestant clergy?

A. "They have, in Massachusetts, at a place called Andover, a kind of minister factory, where each professor takes an oath once in five years—that time being considered the life of an oath—that he has not, during the past five years, and will not, during the next five years, intellectually advance. There is probably no oath that they could easier keep. . . . The professors, for the most part, are ministers who failed in the pulpit and were returned to the seminary on account of their deficiency in reason and their excess of faith" (2:20–21).

Q. Let us turn to another subject. You have frequently referred to "orthodox" Christianity, "orthodox" churches, "orthodox" ministers. What is your understanding of the adjective *Christian?* What do you regard as the "orthodox" view of Christ?

A. "Christ, according to the faith, is the second person in the Trinity, the Father being the first and the Holy Ghost the third. Each of these three persons is God. Christ is his own father and his own son. The Holy Ghost is neither father nor son, but both. The son was begotten by the father, but existed before he was begotten—just the same before as after. Christ is just as old as his father, and the father is just as young as his son. The Holy Ghost proceeded from the Father and Son, but was equal to the Father and Son before he proceeded, that is to say, before he existed, but he is of the same age of the other two.

23

"So it is declared that the Father is God, and the Son God and the Holy Ghost God, and that these three Gods make one God.

"According to the celestial multiplication table, once one is three, and three times one is one, and according to heavenly subtraction if we take two from three, three are left. The addition is equally peculiar, if we add two to one we have but one. Each one is equal to himself and the other two. Nothing ever was, nothing ever can be more perfectly idiotic and absurd than the dogma of the Trinity. . . .

"Think of one of these beings as the father of one, and think of that one as half human and all God, and think of the third as having proceeded from the other two, and then think of all three as one. Think that after the father begot the son, the father was still alone, and after the Holy Ghost proceeded from the father, and the son, the father was still alone—because there never was and never will be but one God.

"At this point, absurdity having reached its limit, nothing more can be said except: 'Let us pray' " (4:266–68).

Q. If that is your understanding of the "orthodox" position, what view of Christ do you hold?

A. "Let me say here, once for all, that for the man Christ I have infinite respect. Let me say, once for all, that the places where man has died for man is holy ground. And let me say, once for all, that to that great and serene man I gladly pay, I gladly pay the tribute of my admiration and my tears. He was a reformer in his day. He was an infidel in his time. He was regarded as a blasphemer, and his life was destroyed by hypocrites, who have, in all ages, done what they could to trample freedom and manhood out of the human mind. Had I lived at that time I would have been his friend, and should he come again he will not find a better friend than I will be.

"That is for the man. For the theological creation I have a different feeling. If he was, in fact, God, he

24

knew there was no such thing as death. He knew that what we called death was but the eternal opening of the golden gates of everlasting life; and it took no heroism to face a death that was eternal life.

"For the man who, in the darkness, said: 'My God, why hast thou forsaken me?'—for that man I have nothing but respect, admiration, and love. Back of the theological shreds, rags, and patches, hiding the real Christ, I see a genuine man" (1:456–58).

Q. How would you describe the "Christian scheme of redemption," as you call it?

A. "According to this scheme, by the sin of Adam and Eve in the Garden of Eden, human nature became evil, corrupt and depraved. It became impossible for human beings to keep, in all things, the law of God. In spite of this, God allowed the people to live and multiply for some fifteen hundred years, and then on account of their wickedness drowned them all with the exception of eight persons.

"The nature of these eight persons was evil, corrupt and depraved, and in the nature of things their children would be cursed with the same nature. Yet God gave them another trial, knowing exactly what the result would be. A few of these wretches he selected and made them objects of his love and care, the rest of the world he gave to indifference and neglect. To civilize the people he had chosen, he assisted them in conquering and killing their neighbors, and gave them the assistance of priests and inspired prophets. For their preservation and punishment he wrought miracles, gave them many laws and a great deal of advice. He taught them to sacrifice oxen, sheep, and doves, to the end that their sins might be forgiven. The idea was inculcated that there was a certain relation between the sin and the sacrifice—the greater the sin, the greater the sacrifice. He also taught the savagery that without the shedding of blood there was no remission of sin.

"In spite of all his efforts, the people grew gradually worse. They would not, they could not keep his laws.

25

"A sacrifice had to be made for the sins of the people. The sins were too great to be washed out by the blood of animals or men. It became necessary for God himself to be sacrificed. . . . In only one way could the guilty be justified, and that was by the death, the sacrifice of the innocent. And the innocent being sacrificed must be great enough to atone for the world. There was but one such being—God.

"Thereupon God took upon himself flesh, was born into the world—was known as Christ—was murdered, sacrificed by the Jews, and became an atonement for the sins of the human race.

"This is the scheme of Redemption—the atonement.

"It is impossible to conceive of anything more utterly absurd" (4:281–83).

"Christianity has sold, and continues to sell, crime on a credit. It has taught, and it still teaches, that there is forgiveness for all. Of course it teaches morality. It says: 'Do not steal, do not murder'; but it adds, 'but if you do both, there is a way of escape: believe on the Lord Jesus Christ and thou shalt be saved.' I insist that such a religion is no restraint. It is far better to teach that there is no forgiveness, and that every human being must bear the consequences of his acts" (6:173).

Q. What would you say to those who speak of America as a "Christian" land?

A. "It is contended by many that ours is a Christian government, founded upon the Bible, and that all who look upon that book as false or foolish are destroying the foundation of our country. The truth is, our government is not founded upon the rights of gods, but upon the rights of men. Our Constitution was framed, not to declare and uphold the deity of Christ, but the sacredness of humanity. Ours is the first government made by the people and for the people. It is the only nation with which the gods have nothing to do. And yet there are some judges dishonest and cowardly enough to solemnly decide that this is a Christian country, and that our free institutions are based upon the infamous laws of Jehovah. Such judges are the Jeffries of the church. They believe that decisions, made by hirelings at the bidding of kings, are binding upon man forever. They regard old law as far superior to modern justice. They are what might be called orthodox judges. . . . No honest court ever did, or ever will, decide that our Constitution is Christian. The Bible teaches that God is the source of all authority, and that all kings have obtained their power from him. Every tyrant has claimed to be the agent of the Most High. The Inquisition was founded, not in the name of man, but in the name of God" (1:199–202).

"As a matter of fact, the infidel has a thousand times more reason to vote against the Christian, than the Christian has to vote against the infidel. The Christian believes in a book superior to the Constitution—superior to all Constitutions and laws. The infidel believes the Constitution and law are superior to any book. He is not controlled by any power beyond the seas or above the clouds. He does not receive his orders from Rome, or Sinai. He receives them from his fellow-citizens, legally and constitutionally expressed" (5:309).

Q. What constructive word can you offer?

A. "Science is the real redeemer. It will put honesty above hypocrisy; mental veracity above all belief. It will teach the religion of usefulness. It will destroy bigotry in all its forms. It will put thoughtful doubt above thoughtless faith. It will give us philosophers, thinkers and savants, instead of priests, theologians and saints. It will abolish poverty and crime, and greater, grander, nobler than all else, it will make the whole world free" (4:349).

"I oppose the church because she is the enemy of liberty; because her dogmas are infamous and cruel; because she humiliates and degrades woman; because she teaches the doctrines of eternal torment and the natural depravity of man; because she resorts to falsehood and slander; because she is arrogant and revengeful; because she allows men to sin on a credit; because she discourages self-reliance, and laughs at good works; because she believes in vicarious virtue and vicarious vice—vicarious punishment and vicarious reward; because she sacrifices the world we have to one we know not of" (1:263).

Ingersoll's description of Christianity as the faith of ignorant people subscribing to an infallible book that reveals an immoral God acting in preposterous ways is entertaining at best. His picture is painted in blacks and whites, and the subtleties and nuances of religious language escape his understanding. Yet his broadside is possible only because of the image of purity that exists so strongly (although not always overtly) in many persons' understanding of the Christian faith.

The Moral Evangelist: The Image of Piety

Another image of the Christian faith in our common understanding is that of piety. By that term I mean an unreflective and uncritical acceptance of moral precepts that are clothed in Christian language and demand heartfelt response and defense. In describing "evangelical Protestantism," William McLoughlin has written:

> The basic ethic of this form of Protestantism
> was in complete harmony with the individual-
> istic, laissez-faire social outlook of the nineteenth
> century. It equated the old Puritan sense of
> mission with the missionary movement at home
> and abroad; through missionaries, revivals, and
> soul-winning preaching, God was gradually
> spreading the gospel and converting the world
> to the Christian (and also the Anglo-Saxon,
> democratic, capitalistic, and American) way of
> life. Essential to this was the Protestant ethic of
> hard work, thrift, piety, and sobriety. In the
> euphoric atmosphere of America's growing

wealth, prestige, and power, the mood of evangelicalism was as optimistic as its morality was Victorian.[15]

To illustrate this somewhat elusive and imprecise image, let us look at Jerry Falwell, a contemporary "moral evangelist." After his religious conversion at age eighteen, Falwell entered and graduated from Baptist Bible College in Springfield, Missouri, and began his ministry at the newly formed Thomas Road Baptist Church in Lynchburg, Virginia. Through his persuasive preaching and use of radio and television, his congregation grew rapidly and today is said to be the second largest church in the country. His "old time religion" on the program "The Old-Time Gospel Hour" met a need for many and served as a beacon around which the "Moral Majority" gathered. Since its founding in 1979 the Moral Majority enlisted "evangelicals" to support conservative political candidates and causes and during the 1980s attracted wide attention. On June 11, 1989, Falwell announced that "our mission is accomplished" and the organization was disbanded.[16] Like other contemporary moral evangelists, Falwell seeks to recall Americans to values that he sees as threatened or disappearing, values that made America great. Secularism, communism, abortion, homosexuality, sex education in public schools, the welfare state, the feminist movement—are all signs of the decay of this Christian land.

It is Falwell's conviction that the "root of America's problems today is the decay of our individual and national morals." A new birth is needed. Why? Because the Christian presupposes the sinfulness of the human self, although moderns persist in their effort to discredit the story of creation and the idea of original sin. "If man is not basically bad; if he is not inherently evil, having received from the fall the very nature of sin and having death passed upon him and all men; if the depravity of man is not a fact from the very fall in the garden, then the death, the burial, and the resurrection of Jesus Christ were needless and worthless."[17] Each and every one of us needs a new birth, which demands an admission of sin (defined in moralistic terms) and the acceptance of Jesus Christ as Savior.

The core of Falwell's analysis of the existing threat to America's future is laid out in the second part, "Morality—The Deciding Factor," of his *Listen, America!* Its sections consider the family, children's rights, the feminist movement, the right to life, homosexuality, television, pornography, education, music, and drugs and alcohol. There is no question where Falwell stands on each. Until the tide of secularism is turned and our historic values recaptured, America will continue to decay. Yet, Falwell insists:

> I do not believe that God is finished with America yet. America has more God-fearing citizens per capita than any other nation on earth. There are millions of Americans who love God, decency, and biblical morality. North America is the last logical base for world evangelization. While it is true that God could use any nation or means possible to spread the Gospel to the world, it is also true that we have the churches, the schools, the young people, the media, the money, and the means of spreading the Gospel worldwide in our lifetime. God loves all the world, not just America. However, I am convinced that our freedoms are essential to world evangelism in this latter part of the twentieth century.

What is his program for evangelism? God's people must show humility, must pray, must "seek the face of God, and must turn from their wicked ways. America has been great because she has been good."[18] And, since America was born in her churches, rebirth must begin there.

Falwell has advertised a "Christian Bill of Rights," a convenient summary of his position and a good example of the message of the contemporary moral evangelist.

Amendment I   We believe that, from the time of conception within the womb, every human being has a scriptural right to life upon this earth. (Exod. 20:13; Ps. 139:13-16)

Amendment II   We believe that every person has the right to pursue any and all scriptural goals that he or she feels are God-directed during that life upon this earth. (Prov. 3:5-6)

Amendment III   We believe that, apart from justified capital punishment, no medical or judicial process should be introduced that would allow the termination of life before its natural or accidental completion. (Ps. 31:15)

Amendment IV   We believe that no traitorous verbal or written attack upon this beloved nation advocating overthrow by force be permitted by any citizen or alien living within this country. (Rom. 13:1-7)

Amendment V   We believe that all students enrolled in public schools should have the right to voluntary prayer and Bible reading. (Josh. 24:15)

Amendment VI   We believe in the right and responsibility to establish and administer private Christian schools without harassment from local, state, or federal government. (Deut. 11:18-21)

Amendment VII   We believe in the right to influence secular professions, including the fields

of politics, business, legal, medical, in establishing and maintaining moral principles of
Scripture. (Prov. 14:34)

Amendment VIII   We believe in the right to
expect our national leaders to keep this country
morally and militarily strong so that religious
freedom and Gospel preaching might continue
unhindered. (1 Pet. 2:13-17)

Amendment IX   We believe in the right to
receive moral support from all local, state, and
federal agencies concerning the traditional family
unit, a concept that enjoys both scriptural and
historical precedence. (Gen. 2:18-25)

Amendment X   We believe in the right of
legally approved religious organizations to main-
tain their tax-exempt status, this right being
based upon the historical and scriptural concept
of church and state separation. (Matt. 22:17-21)

Falwell's advertisement promises, "In return for your
support I will send a beautiful parchment reproduction
of the Christian Bill of Rights along with an 'Old Glory'
lapel pin for you to proudly wear."[19]

This evangelical call to moral renewal is without
any touch of ambiguity. The moral principles which
need to be recaptured are self-evident and biblical. This
call to moral reformation, which has been the hallmark
of the evangelist, presupposes that reformation of the
individual will bring reformation of society, not vice
versa. On this point the moral evangelists differ fundamentally from those involved in the Social Gospel in
the earlier part of the twentieth century. For Walter Raus-
chenbusch, Washington Gladden, and other leaders of
the Social Gospel, reformation of society will bring reformation of individuals. Social reform movements
therefore became their focus. Both the moral evangelist
and the advocate of the Social Gospel presupposed "the

right and the good"; each believed the turnabout was possible and the end unambiguous.

It is from the inheritance of revivalism and most particularly the moral evangelist that the image of piety is derived. The Christian is one who in his or her heart believes that the Bible contains the specific moral precepts that should guide not only one's moral life but also the mission of our nation itself.

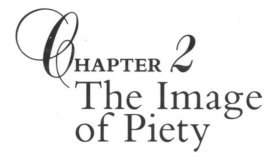

CHAPTER 2

The Image
of Piety

Our working definition of the image of piety is "an unreflective and uncritical acceptance of moral precepts that are clothed in Christian language and demand heartfelt response and defense." The term *Pietism* has more specific reference to the broad movement in Western Christianity that was expressed in the Moravian movement in the Lutheran churches of Germany, the Wesleyan revivals in Anglicanism in England, and the Great Awakening in America—all of which, interestingly, occurred at approximately the same time in the eighteenth century. It is an "exceedingly difficult movement to define," Sydney Ahlstrom wrote, but his description is useful.

It was an effort to intensify Christian piety and
purity of life. At the outset it also involved a
protest against intellectualism, churchly
formalism, and ethical passivity. With the
passing decades this protest broadened; pietists
also began to inveigh against the new forms of
rationalism and the spiritual coldness of the
Enlightenment. Pietism was thus a movement of
revival, aimed at making man's relation to God
experientially and morally meaningful as well as

socially relevant. It stressed the feelings of the
heart. It emphasized the royal priesthood and
sought to revive the laity. It called always for a
return to the Bible.[1]

Certainly this movement has had a profound effect on
the understanding of modern Christianity. Though the
image of piety stems from Pietism, it does not have the
theological *content* that one finds in the English Methodist
John Wesley, in the Moravian Count Zinzendorf, or even
in the American revivalist Charles Grandison Finney.
William McLoughlin has written extensively on Pietism in America and was influenced by Ernst Troeltsch[2]
and H. Richard Niebuhr.[3] McLoughlin noted a distinction between "mystical or quietistic Pietism" and activ-
istic "pietistic-perfectionism," the former largely European and the latter English and American. In
McLoughlin's words:

> It was not the forest or the free land, however,
> which broke down those remnants of the Euro-
> pean civilization which the pietists brought with
> them. What broke down the stratified class
> system, the established church, the mercantile
> economic practices, the corporate concept of
> society, was the internal dynamic of pietistic-
> perfectionism itself. For there is an inherent
> tension within pietism, as well as between the
> varieties of pietism that came to America, which
> has generated a continual spirit of reformation, a
> constant search for a more perfect union
> between God and man in America from the
> outset. . . . [I see it] as a conflict between the
> conservative and the antinomian aspects of
> pietism—between those whose primary concern
> is to maintain perfect moral order and those
> whose primary concern is to attain perfect moral
> freedom. . . . The concept of the omnicompe-
> tent, self-governing, self-reliant common man

was really the final triumph of the first stage of American pietistic perfectionism. In the Age of Jackson the two interacting components of pietistic perfectionism flowered in unison: inner perfection or holiness as personal union with God and the perfectibility of the world through the regeneration of everyone in it. America had at last thrown off all the shackles of Satan and all the carnal corruptions of this world and was now ready for the ultimate confrontation with God. In 1836 Charles Grandison Finney, the foremost evangelist of his day and later president of Oberlin College in its perfectionist era, predicted that it would be possible to convert "the whole land in two years."

This became a dominant mood of much of mainline Protestantism in the nineteenth century, and revivalistic measures became the means of persuading others. McLoughlin continues:

> Evangelical Protestant denominations became a kind of national church dedicated to enforcing the moral law upon everyone in the nation either by revivalistic religion (which produced voluntary obedience) or by a majority vote of the regenerate (which compelled obedience of the unregenerate). However, in their zeal to make America a Christian country the evangelicals began to equate the moral absolute with their own narrow set of Protestant, middle-class, rural virtues. They wanted to outlaw the Masons and the Mormons, to enact nativist laws, to enforce prohibition, to censor immorality, to prevent birth control, to maintain a Christian sabbath, and eventually to restrict immigration and pass laws preventing the teaching of evolution.[4]

The agenda described by McLoughlin is remarkably similar to the "Christian Bill of Rights" of the moral evangelist Jerry Falwell.

The assumption underlying this attitude was based on an Arminian, or incipiently Pelagian, view of human nature. With Pietism came an increasingly specific understanding of the nature of the Christian life. Inner perfection is possible for oneself; inner perfection is also possible for others. (Not until the nineteenth century was the image of the Puritan changed into one who is puritanical; Nathaniel Hawthorne's *Scarlet Letter* had more than a little to do with this transformation. The Pietist, not the Puritan, is puritanical.)

The Roots of Pietism

One can argue that the most important theological issue in this image of Christianity is the nature of the human self: the human capacity for good and the nature of sin. The Pietist presupposed a certain understanding of this problem, and to clarify it we look briefly at how the issue has been interpreted in Christian history.

In his Letter to the Romans Paul was addressing the issue of the relation of the law to Jew and Gentile. His words have prompted many debates and continue to confound interpreters. What is the role of "law"? What is the gospel in relation to law? Paul wrote:

> For what I do is not what I want to do, but
> what I detest. But if what I do is against my
> will, it means that I agree with the law and hold
> it to be admirable. But as things are, it is no
> longer I who perform the action, but sin that
> lodges in me. For I know that nothing good
> lodges in me—in my unspiritual nature, I
> mean—for though the will to do good is there,
> the deed is not. The good which I want to do, I
> fail to do; but what I do is the wrong which is

against my will; and if what I do is against my will, clearly it is no longer I who am the agent, but sin that has its lodging in me. (Rom. 7:15-20, NEB)

Who then is the agent? Is it me or is it my nature, which is somehow other than my will? In debate the issue became hardened, and the elasticity of Paul's own formulations became lost.

Much of the debate through the centuries has been shaped by the controversy between St. Augustine (354–430) and Pelagius (c. 360–c. 420). (Note that Augustine, not Pelagius, has the title *saint.*) Their debate is complex and cannot be fully unraveled here, but it is worth noting what seems to have been the crux of the issue. Augustine was convinced that the Pelagians were mistakenly defending free will and "hastening to a confidence rather in doing righteousness of free-will than of God's aid, and so that every one may glory in himself, and not in the Lord."[5] Pelagius, on the other hand, wrote:

> We are not defending natural goodness in such a way as to say that it is not able to do evil; we emphatically say that it is capable of good and evil. We are only defending our nature against this one affront [i.e., the charge of evil by natural necessity] so that at least we will not seem to be impelled toward evil by that particular blemish—we who do neither good nor evil without our will. To us it is always open to do one of the two, since we are always able to do both.[6]

Because of the "fall of Adam," Augustine insisted that without faith, a gift of grace, the effect of sin (a singular term) is unremitting. To Pelagius even free will is a sign of God's grace, and through that gift one can avoid sins (a plural term). The debate between them was in part

38

flawed because the key words had different meanings; it is not that Augustine believed in the sinfulness of the human being and Pelagius insisted on the goodness of the human, but that is the way the debate has frequently been interpreted.

Throughout the early and high Middle Ages the issue resurfaced, and the debate was no less confusing. In the sixteenth and seventeenth centuries, however, the issue became clearer, perhaps because statements of the positions were less ambiguous. The heirs of John Calvin (1509–64) and James Arminius (1560–1609) focused the issue sharply. Calvin, the premier systematic theologian of the Protestant Reformation, had been trained as a lawyer, and his legal mind had influence on his theology: he developed the implications of his premises.

Calvin believed that the sin of Adam has been inherited by the human race and that all are now in their natural state separated from God. The only way in which the separation between the human and God can be overcome and salvation achieved is through the sheer grace and mercy of the sovereign Lord of the Universe. The only way that salvation can be explained, given the sinful state of the human, is that God elects or predestines those whom God will. There is no health within us; how else can the possibility of salvation be understood?

> In conformity, therefore, to the clear doctrine of the Scripture, we assert, that by an eternal and immutable counsel, God has once for all determined, both whom he would admit to salvation, and whom he would condemn to destruction. We affirm that this counsel, as far as concerns the elect, is founded on his gratuitous mercy, totally irrespective of human merit; but that to those whom he devotes to condemnation, the gate of life is closed by a just and irreprehensible, but incomprehensible, judgment.[7]

39

What an unambiguous statement! Calvin begins with an arbitrary, sovereign God, the creator of all that is; rebellion has occurred, and punishment ensues. How else, he reasons, can one possibly explain the conviction of election than by predestination, an affirmation that this sovereign God is also merciful? Calvin's disciples carried his argument along and prompted a controversy between the supralapsarian and infralapsarian Calvinists.

James Arminius, professor of theology at Leyden, Holland, became involved in the developing controversy concerning the interpretation of Calvinism. As a member of the Dutch Reformed Church, he was asked to respond to the attacks on supralapsarian Calvinism circulated by Dirck Coornhert (1522–90). The supralapsarian position affirmed that God decreed the election of some and the reprobation of others and then permitted the fall as the means by which the divine decree would be carried out. The infralapsarians theorized that God permitted the fall and then decreed that some would be elected and others damned. In developing his position against those who were attacking supralapsarian Calvinism, Arminius became convinced by a less severe Calvinism than he had previously held. As a result he was himself attacked by a leader of the supralapsarian school, Franz Gomarus (1563–1641). Out of this controversy grew the school of Calvinism known as Arminianism.

Arminius placed an emphasis on human responsibility and action but not to the exclusion of an emphasis on the grace of God.

> This is my opinion concerning the Free-will of man: In his primitive condition as he came out of the hands of his Creator, man was endowed with such a portion of knowledge, holiness and power, as enabled him to understand, esteem, consider, will, and to perform The True Good, according to the commandment delivered to him. Yet none of these acts could he do, except

through the assistance of Divine Grace. But in his lapsed and sinful state, man is not capable, of and by himself, either to think, to will, or to do that which is really good; but it is necessary for him to be regenerated and renewed in his intellect, affections or will, and in all his powers, by God in Christ through the Holy Spirit, that he may be qualified rightly to understand, esteem, consider, will, and perform whatever is truly good. When he is made a partaker of this regeneration or renovation, I consider that, since he is delivered from sin, he is capable of thinking, willing and doing that which is good, but yet not without the continued aid of Divine Grace.[8]

The Pietist movement of the eighteenth and nineteenth centuries was rooted in this Arminian view of human nature. John Wesley (1703–91) was the theological leader of this movement, though his theology was more in the form of pastoral addresses than theological essays. Certainly he was troubled by Calvinism and the doctrine of predestination. In 1765 he wrote, "Just so my brother and I reasoned thirty years ago: 'We think it our duty to oppose predestination with our whole strength, not as an opinion, but as a dangerous mistake which appears to be subversive of the very foundations of Christian experience and which has, in fact, given occasion to the most grievous offences.' "[9] His Arminian assumptions led him to assert the notion of "Christian perfection," a term that was later misused or misinterpreted by many American Methodists.[10] Wesley wrote, "In conformity, therefore, both to the doctrine of St. John, and to the whole tenor of the New Testament, we fix this conclusion: *a Christian is so far perfect as not to commit sin.*"[11] But perfection is a process and not a state at which one arrives, an important qualification. Certainly Wesley's words would frequently give a Calvinist heartburn, but Wesley was convinced that the harsher aspects of Calvinism were unscriptural; on the issue of justification by faith, however, he wrote: "I think on justification just as I have done any time these seven and twenty years, and just as Mr. Calvin does. In this respect I do not differ from him an hair's breadth."[12] But many Wesleyans later did. To put it briefly, Wesley was insisting that there is a role for the human will, and yet he never underestimated the centrality of grace, whether prevenient, sanctifying, or sacramental. The image of piety derives from this root, but its emphasis has changed.

Revivalism and the Millennium

The revivalism of nineteenth-century American Protestantism gave an increasing emphasis to human action and responsibility and began to emphasize the works of the righteous. Charles Grandison Finney (1792–1875) was a transitional figure, one of the most popular and influential voices in the first half of the nineteenth century. He had studied law with a lawyer in upper New York State and then theology with George Gale, a Presbyterian from Princeton. After he was licensed to preach in 1824 he conducted revivals in New York State. During the next decade he became involved in the controversies stemming from the work of Nathaniel William Taylor, the noted professor of theology at Yale. Taylor, an heir of the New Divinity, or Edwardsean/Calvinist tradition, in New England theology, had confronted the increasingly loud voices of Unitarianism. He attempted to develop a position defending Calvinism yet responding to the increasing call for self-determination of the will. Taylor and Finney began with the Arminian premise of self-determination, and not with the Calvinistic premise of the sovereignty and arbitrariness of God. The outcome was inevitable. As a noted revivalist, much in demand and in the public view, he received attention as the inventor of the "anxious bench," literally a bench placed in the front of the church just beneath the pulpit and designed for those who were on the fence about conversion. Finney directed his remarks straight to them, and the results were notable.

One of Finney's sermons was entitled "Sinners Bound to Change Their Own Hearts." (Note the contrast of the title with Jonathan Edwards's "Sinners in the Hands of an Angry God," preached toward the end of the First Great Awakening in October 1741, in Enfield, Connecticut.) Finney's sermon had as its text, "Make you a new heart and a new spirit" (Ezek. 18:31).

> How is this requirement to "make yourself a new heart" consistent with the often repeated declarations of the Bible, that a new heart is the gift and work of God[?] . . . The fact is, that the actual turning, or change, is the sinner's own act. The agent who induces him, is the Spirit of God. A secondary agent is the preacher, or individual who presents the truth. The truth is the instrument or motive which the Spirit uses to induce the sinner to turn. Suppose yourself to be standing on the bank of the Falls of Niagara. As you stand upon the verge of the precipice, you behold a man lost in reverie, approaching its verge unconscious of its danger. He approaches nearer and nearer until he actually lifts his foot to take the final step that shall plunge him into destruction. At that moment you lift your warning voice above the roar of the foaming waters and cry out—Stop. The voice pierces his ear, and breaks the charm that binds him; he turns instantly upon his heel, all pale and aghast he retires, quivering, from the verge of death. He reels and almost swoons with horror; turns and walks slowly to the public house; you follow him; the manifest agitation in his countenance calls numbers around him; and on your approach he points to you and says—that man saved my life. Here he ascribes the work to you; and certainly there is a sense in which you saved

him. But, on being further questioned he says,
Stop, how that word rings in my ears. Oh, that
was to me the word of life. Here he ascribes it
to that word that aroused him, and caused him
to turn. But, on conversing further, he said, had
I not turned at that instant I should have been a
dead man. Here he speaks of it, and truly, as his
own act.[13]

The turning about is one's own act. This is Arminianism, incipient Pelagianism, pure and simple. This
changing view of human nature as seen in the developing
Pietist emphases shaped much of mainline Protestantism
in nineteenth- and twentieth-century America, as much
as did "the quality of pragmatism or of democratic liberalism or the influence of the frontier."[14]

The means for spreading the faith was persuasion,
which took the form of revivalism. Camp meetings were
held not only to alleviate isolation in an expanding nation
but also to convert souls. And the camp meeting sermon
focused on the hanky-panky going on behind the circle
of wagons, not on the interpretation of Scripture or a
chapter of the Westminster Confession. The focus of
church life changed. Church records of the seventeenth
and eighteenth centuries referred to congregational discussions of the interpretation of scriptural passages and
doctrinal issues; even Puritan divines were cited. What
greater test could there be of sophistication and literacy!
But frequently the minutes of Baptist and Methodist
churches in the Western Reserve focused on other issues.
For example, the Elkhorn Baptist Church in Kentucky
recorded the following:

> *The 2nd Saturday in November 1804*
> Excluded Hannah Day's wife for swearing
> and keeping another man besides her husband;
> James Major was excluded from the Church for
> intoxication and shooting for liquor; Brother
> Red Major came before the Church and was

dealt with for Shooting for liquor and the Church directed the moderator to give him a word of admonition. Robert Hicklin was excluded from the Church for horse racing.

2nd Saturday in March 1805
A charge was brought against Sister Polly Edrington for frequently giving her Mother the lie, & calling her a fool and for indeavouring by tattling to set several of the Neighbors at strife with each other. She was excluded for the same.
Charges brought against Br. James Major for saying that John Dupey slapt him in the face & he drawd himself up and bore it.[15]

Two other strands of the Pietist movement characterized its development in the nineteenth century: perfectionism and millennialism. Given the Pietists' presupposition concerning human nature—Arminianism verging on Pelagianism—it was but a short step to the notion that it was possible to become perfect on earth. To a Calvinist, this idea was sheer blasphemy, but not to the Oberlin school of thought under the leadership of Charles Finney and Asa Mahan. Finney and Mahan embraced perfectionist notions, and Oberlin became noted for this emphasis. To be sure, the perfectionism of Finney and Mahan was more moderate than that of John Humphrey Noyes and his communitarian experiment at Oneida, New York, where goods, wives, husbands, and children were held in common—yet perfectionism it was. In his *Memoirs* Finney wrote:

One of our theological students arose, and put the inquiry, whether the Gospel did not provide for Christians, all the conditions of an established faith and hope and love; . . . in short whether sanctification was not attainable in this life; that is sanctification in such a sense that Christians could have unbroken peace, and not

45

come into condemnation, or have the feeling of condemnation or a consciousness of sin. Brother Mahan immediately answered "YES."[16]

These individuals were not suggesting that a state of complete perfection could be achieved in this life, but it could be approached. "Holiness, in a creature, may also be perfect, and yet progressive—progressive, not in its nature but in degree. . . . He is perfect in holiness, whose love at each successive moment corresponds with the extent of his powers."[17] In other words, through diligence and struggle, one could expect to come closer with each passing day to fulfilling the biblical injunction, "Be perfect, as your heavenly Father is perfect" (Matt. 5:48). That call appealed to many and provided the motive for what may properly be called works righteousness.

It must be noted that Finney was not an extremist. He deplored fanaticism and would not be sympathetic with some of the techniques of the televangelists of the 1980s. One example will suffice.

I attended a camp meeting in the State of New York which had been in progress two or three days before my arrival. I heard the preachers and attended the exercises through most of that day, and there appeared to be very little—indeed no visible excitement. After several sermons had been preached and after much exhortation, prayer and singing, I observed several of the leading men to be whispering to each other for some time as if in profound deliberation, after which one of them, a man of athletic frame and stentorian voice, came down from the stand and pressed his way along into the midst of a company of women who were sitting in front of the stand, and then began to clap his hands and halloo at the top of his voice: power! power!! power!!!. Soon, another and another set in, till there was a general shouting and clapping of hands, followed presently by the shrieking of women, and resulting after a little time in the falling of several of them from their seats. Then it was proclaimed that the power of God was revealed from heaven. After pushing the excitement to a most extraordinary extent, the minister who began it and those who united with him and had thus succeeded as they supposed in bringing down the power of God upon the congregation, retired from the scene of confusion manifestly much gratified at the result.

This scene and some others of a similar character have often occurred to my mind . . . things often occur in revivals which seem to beget an excitement but little more intelligent than this. Such appeals are made to the imagination and to certain departments of the sensibility as completely to throw the action of the intellect into the shade. So far as such efforts to promote revivals are made, they are undoubtedly highly disastrous, and should be entirely discouraged.[18]

Although Finney recognized the extremes of the revivals, the very fact that the extremes occurred helped to shape the image of piety.[19]

The millennial theme, too, has a long history in Christian life and thought.[20] Basically there are two types, pre- and post-millennialism. Pre-millennialists believe that Christ's return inaugurates the millennium, the thousand-year reign of peace; post-millennialists believe that the millennium has begun or will soon begin and will culminate in the return of Christ. In the United States, the most vocal if not the majority strain is pre-millennialist. Jonathan Edwards, a post-millennialist, saw signs of the beginning of the millennium in the period of the Great Awakening.

William Miller, a pre-millennialist, through an examination of Scripture, stated that Christ would return to earth in 1843. Apparently nothing happened, he went back to the Bible, and revised the date to October 22, 1844. Miller vividly described what was to happen.

> I am satisfied that the end of the world is at
> hand. The evidence flows in from every quarter.
> . . . Soon, very soon God will arise in his anger
> and the vine of the earth will be reaped. See!
> See!—the angel with his sharp sickle is about to
> take the field! See yonder trembling victims fall
> before his pestilential breath! . . . The heavens
> grow black with clouds; the sun has veiled
> himself; the moon, pale and forsaken, hangs in
> middle air; the hail descends; the seven thunders
> utter loud their voices; the lightnings send their
> vivid gleams and sulphurous flames abroad; and
> the great city of the nations falls to rise no more
> forever and forever! at this dread moment, look!
> The clouds have burst asunder; the heavens
> appear; the great white throne is in sight!
> Amazement fills the Universe with awe! He
> comes!—He comes!—Behold the Saviour
> comes!—Lift up your heads, ye saints—He
> comes! He comes! He comes![21]

The millennium was about to begin.

These changing emphases affected the training of clergy. In the seventeenth and eighteenth centuries would-be clergy had rigorous training, even though theological seminaries did not appear until the nineteenth century. For example, Jonathan Edwards entered Yale College in 1716, at the age of thirteen. By then he had already studied the classics and was well versed in Greek and Latin. In the first year of the Yale curriculum time was given to language training in Greek, Hebrew, and Latin. The second year was devoted to "Languages, Logick, Rhetoric, Oratory, Geography and Natural Philosophy." The third year dealt with "most branches of

Mathematics, Natural Philosophy," and for many, "Surveying, Navigation and the Calculation of Eclipses." And the last year was devoted to "Metaphysics, Ethicks, and Divinity."[22] After graduation the student frequently spent some months with a settled parson, similar to the way one studied law. Joseph Bellamy, a New England parson, trained at least sixty of these students before their ordination.[23]

The Pietist churches of the nineteenth century, especially the Baptists and Methodists, however, did not require such rigorous training. The autobiography of Jacob Bower, a frontier Baptist preacher and missionary, is a fascinating account of his life before his ordination.

> I was born in Manheim Township, Lancaster county in the State of Pennsylvania, on the 26. day of September in the year of our Lord 1786. When I was about three years old my Father emigrated to what was then called the backwoods of Westmorland county. Early in the month of May before I was six years old I was sent to a German school, and by the time I was six years old, I could read the New Testament.
>
> Thank God for pious parents.
>
> . . . My parents belonged to the denomination of Christians called Tunkers, as early as I can recollect, my Father kept up regular morning and evening worship in the family. Commonly he would read a chapter in the German Testament, then sing a hymn in German, then say a prayer in the same language, and we were taught to sing with them. We were instructed in such lessons as we were able to understand, such as this. Be good children, all good children when they die will go to a good place, wher Jesus is, and many pretty Angels, and they would be happy forever. Bad children when they die will go to a bad place, where there is a

great fire, and the Devil and his Angels
tormenting the wicked forever. These instruc-
tions were ingraven on my mind, I have never
forgotten them, and were a means of continual
restraint from being wicked. In January after I
was six years old, the Lord took my good
Mother home to Heaven, and I wished very
much to go withe her to the good place she had
gon to. . . . Sometime in July following, my
Father brought home a step Mother, and it was
not long before my anxiety to die increased
more and more. . . . I lived a farasee, trusting in
my good name, and innocence, till I was in my
nineteenth year. [Bower then fell under the
influence of a Universalist preacher; he became
worried about his faith and his soul.] But the
ever memorable morning of the 17th day of
December 1811. About 2 oclock A.M. when
most people were in their beds sound asleep.
There was an Earthquake, verry violent indeed.
. . . I expected immediate destruction, had no
hope of seeing the dawn of another day. Eternity, oh eternity was just at hand, and all of us
unprepared. . . . To see everything touching the
earth, shakeing—quivering,trembling; and mens
hearts quaking for fear of the approaching judgment.

After a period of searching, Bower joined a Baptist community, began preaching, with "no books beside my
English Bible & a German Testament, and a small hymn
book," and was ordained by the Hazle Creek Church.[24]
With such requirements of preparation there was no
shortage of male clergy for the Pietist churches; the role
of women, however, in leadership roles was not yet
developed.[25]
    When the theme of perfectionism is tied together
with the theme of millennialism, we have a potent con-
coction. Prepare now, for He is about to come—soon,

soon, soon! In the Pietist sense, you can become perfect—morally upright, "good." It is up to you. But, as
ample numbers of clergy warned, it is later than you
think.

The Gospel of Wealth

Another element of this image of piety is related to
the themes of revivalism, perfectionism, and millennialism and may be called "inverted Puritanism" or works
righteousness. According to this view, the just shall be
known by their fruits, or, in the words of the Massachusetts Episcopal bishop, William Lawrence, ". . . in
the long run, it is only to the man of morality that wealth
comes."[26] This "gospel of wealth" expressed the conviction of many and can be seen as an outgrowth of
Calvinism. Calvin and Calvinists sought to justify works
in relation to the fundamental principle of justification
by faith and the notion of predestination. If one is redeemed by the sole, arbitrary action of a sovereign God,
what role does human action have? Certainly not to bring
about redemption. But Calvin did write, "In the elect,
we consider calling as an evidence of election, and justification as another token of its manifestation, till they
arrive in glory, which constitutes its completion."[27]
One's vocation and the way it is fulfilled are signs of
election, not its cause. The New England Puritan followed that argument. The catch phrase attributed to
Anne Hutchinson, "Sanctification is no evidence of justification," prompted the antinomian controversy in the
1630s in Massachusetts. Hutchinson, arguing from
strong Calvinistic premises, insisted that works are not
necessarily signs of election, and the Puritan fathers had
to agree. (Anne was declared a heretic because of her
claim to an inner revelation, not because of her position
on justification and sanctification.) The "gospel of
wealth," however, altered this basic thrust with different
presuppositions about human nature.

Russell Conwell (1843–1925), a lawyer, graduate of Yale, and later pastor of the Grace Baptist Church in Philadelphia, was an outspoken advocate of this position. His address "Acres of Diamonds" was given over five thousand times and expressed what must have been sweet words to many.

> Now then, I say again that the opportunity to get rich, to attain unto great wealth, is here in Philadelphia now, within the reach of almost every man and woman who hears me speak to-night, and I mean just what I say. I have not come to this platform even under these circumstances to recite something to you. I have come to tell you what in God's sight I believe to be the truth, and if the years of life have been of any value to me in the attainment of common sense, I know I am right; that the men and women sitting here, who found it difficult perhaps to buy a ticket to this lecture or gathering to-night, have within their reach "acres of diamonds," opportunities to get largely wealthy. There never was a place on earth more adapted than the city of Philadelphia to-day, and never in the history of the world did a poor man without capital have such an opportunity to get rich quickly and honestly as he has now in our city. I say it is the truth, and I want you to accept it as such; for if you think I have come to recite something, then I would better not be here. I have no time to waste in any such talk, but to say the things I believe, and unless some of you get richer for what I am saying to-night my time is wasted. . . . Is there opportunity to get rich in Philadelphia? Well, now, how simple a thing it is to see where it is, and the instant you see where it is, it is yours. Some old gentleman gets up back there and says, "Mr. Conwell, have you lived in Philadelphia for thirty-one years,

and don't know that the time has gone by when
you can make anything in this city?" "No, I
don't think it is." "Yes, it is; I have tried it."
"What business are you in?" "I kept a store here
for twenty years, and never made over a thousand dollars in the whole twenty years."

"Well, then, you can measure the good you
have been to this city by what this city has paid
you, because a man can judge very well what he
is worth by what he receives; that is, in what he
is to the world at this time. If you have not
made over a thousand dollars in twenty years in
Philadelphia, it would have been better for Philadelphia if they had kicked you out of the city
nineteen years and nine months ago. A man has
no right to keep a store in Philadelphia twenty
years and not make at least five thousand
dollars, even though it be a corner grocery store
up-town." You say, "you cannot make five
thousand dollars in a store now." Oh, my
friends, if you will just take only four blocks
around you, and find out what the people want
and what you ought to supply and set them
down with your pencil, and figure up the profits
you would make if you did supply them, you
would very soon see it. There is wealth right
within the sound of your voice.[28]

Wealth comes to the person of morality; poverty is
the result of sin. That is the gospel of wealth. Such a
view is inverted, if not perverted, Puritanism because
its motivation has become fundamentally different. The
Conwells, the Lawrences, the Carnegies sought wealth
for themselves and to make it available to others, although the latter was almost an afterthought. Stephen
Foster, in his study of the Puritan social ethic in sev-
enteenth-century New England, has summarized the
Puritan notion of stewardship and the view of wealth.

It all came down to a matter of motives. [John] Preston [a Puritan divine] understood the difference between the Protestant ethic and the spirit of capitalism with a subtlety and exactness that would have delighted [Max] Weber: "God makes us rich, by being diligent in our callings, using it to his glory and more good, he doth cast Riches on us. Man makes himselfe rich, when as he makes riches the end of his calling, and doth not expect them as a reward that comes from God."[29]

Diligence in one's calling for the glory of God, not for the acquisition of goods, was the motive behind the Puritan's ethic. The root of the gospel of wealth was different from the theological underpinnings of Puritanism, and nowhere was this difference more evident than in its presuppositions concerning human nature. As Cotton Mather said, "Religion begat prosperity, and the daughter devoured the mother."[30]

The image of piety is many-colored. It views the Christian faith as moralistic and accepts moral admonitions as inherently true and unambiguous, believing that it requires little analysis to recognize and apply virtues such as goodness, kindness, benevolence, and charity. Although relying on biblical texts drawn largely from the Gospels and the Prophets, piety is largely devoid of critical reflection. It believes that Christians can bring about the kingdom of God on earth (if not in this generation, then soon), if only we would devote all our energies and innate abilities into doing so. "Would that it were so easy," Paul, Augustine, Luther, and Calvin might respond.

CHAPTER 3
The Image
of Purity

In a casual conversation some years ago a colleague, a noted anthropologist with impeccable credentials, commented that anyone who did not believe in a historical Adam and Eve was not a Christian. Raised as a Southern Baptist, he had long since distanced himself from any relation to the Christian church, yet he retained the image of purity, the notion that there are definite beliefs that a Christian must hold. Frequently these have been summed up as five inviolate points: (1) the inspiration and inerrancy of the Bible, (2) the deity of Christ and his virgin birth, (3) the substitutionary atonement of Christ, (4) the literal resurrection of Christ from the dead, and (5) the literal return of Christ.[1] To deny any one is to deny them all. Where does this image come from?

The Rise of Fundamentalism

In the late nineteenth and early part of the twentieth centuries, heresy trials in the mainline Protestant denominations were not uncommon; today there are few. George Shriver's *American Religious Heretics* described five of these trials that created lengthy ecclesiastical debates and received widespread coverage in the national

55

press.[2] Recently, however, newspapers only cover the annual debates within the Southern Baptist Convention over the choice of moderator, a perennial battle between those who are "conservative" and those who are "less conservative," and the conflicts within the Missouri Synod of the Lutheran church. Some lament that there is no longer sufficient cause for heresy trials. According to Francis Schaeffer, "The Church is to judge whether a man is a Christian on the basis of his doctrine, the propositional content of his faith, and then his credible profession of faith."[3] Another conservative, Harold Lindsell, bemoaned the fact that John Hick, the editor of *The Myth of God Incarnate,* a volume that "argued Jesus is not God," was admitted to the San Gabriel Presbytery, despite his "unitarianism." Yet for Lindsell, "Whosoever denies the deity of Christ cannot be regenerate, that is, cannot be a Christian."[4] Although the frequency of ecclesiastical debates over points of doctrine has decreased, the image of purity persists.

The term *fundamentalism,* often used in a pejorative sense, is part of our lexicon. George Marsden, whose work has helped us to understand this movement, offers a useful description. "Fundamentalism was a loose, diverse, and changing federation of co-belligerents united by their fierce opposition to modernist attempts to bring Christianity into line with modern thought." He elaborates: "While militancy against modernism was the *key distinguishing* factor that drew fundamentalists together, militancy was not necessarily the *central* trait of fundamentalists. Missions, evangelism, prayer, personal holiness, or a variety of doctrinal concerns may often or usually have been their first interest. Yet, without militancy, none of these important aspects of the movement set it apart as 'fundamentalist.' "[5]

To understand fundamentalism we must see this conservative movement over against the concerns of liberal theology or, even more specifically, modernism. A brief look at the positions of Shailer Mathews (1863–

1941) and J. Gresham Machen (1881–1937) will focus the issue.

Mathews, a graduate of Colby College, received his graduate training at the University of Chicago, where he later became professor of historical theology and dean of the Divinity School; he also served as president of the American (Northern) Baptist Convention and president of the Federal Council of Churches. In his book *The Faith of Modernism,* published in 1924, he defined a modernist as one who "uses the methods of modern science to find, state and use the permanent and central values of inherited orthodoxy in meeting the needs of the modern world." For Mathews, the tools of modern science as applied to theology were biblical criticism, historical studies, and sociology. The task was to examine the sources of the tradition to find and state its central values, namely, the teachings of Jesus Christ and "the inner faith of a century-long movement rather than the formulas in which aspects of this faith were authoritatively expressed." Mathews described modernists as "evangelical Christians" who "accept Jesus Christ as the revelation of a Savior God." In essence, "The Christianity to which the world has always appealed is more than a system of doctrines. *It is a moral and spiritual movement, born of the experience of God known through Jesus Christ as Savior. It is a community of life, not a system of philosophy or theology.*"[6]

The difference between the modernist and the "dogmatic theologian," to use Mathews's term, was not in one's allegiance to the Bible but in the "method of using it and the presuppositions with which it is studied." The Bible contains scientific errors, but "Belief in the providence of God can be expressed in poetry, folk-tale and legend just as truly as in literal statement."[7] Modernists believe not in inerrancy but in the inspiration of the writers of the Bible. In an autobiographical statement Mathews made clear his difficulty with "dogmatic orthodoxy."

> As a result of historical critical study the Bible had already lost its authority as an infallible

revelation to be used as a theological oracle, but now the basis of religious loyalty itself was subject to examination. If one accepted evangelical orthodoxy it could only be because of the authority of a group or a literature rather than because of any demonstration of its truth. But if the decisions of the group themselves were functional, a method by which the social mind of a given period adapted religion for its own good, what was there left of Christianity for our own day? The only answer that I could see would be that ecclesiastical authority must be replaced by some intelligible method by which one would be able to distinguish between the form and the content of an inherited religious group belief, and then determine as to the truth of its content by such criteria as were applicable.[8]

To the modernists, or liberals, the Bible was not self-authenticating; criteria external to it were to be followed. Mathews could use some of the same biblical words as did the conservatives, referring, for example, to Jesus as Savior and to resurrection and divine revelation, but his meanings were not the same.

A year earlier, in 1923, J. Gresham Machen published *Christianity and Liberalism*. Though Machen disavowed the fundamentalist label, he was certainly one of the most learned and outspoken opponents of liberalism and its methodology. He had studied at Johns Hopkins and Princeton Seminary and also at centers of theological study in Germany: Marburg and Göttingen. He was a defender of Reformed theology. Even at the bastion of Calvinist orthodoxy, Princeton Theological Seminary, he could not find a comfortable home and so, in 1929, left to found Westminster Theological Seminary and the Orthodox Presbyterian Church. In defending his departure from Princeton Seminary, he wrote that he belonged to the "ancient yet living tradition of the old Princeton. I hold (1) that the Christian religion, as

58

it is set forth on the basis of Holy Scripture in the Standards of the Reformed Faith, is true, and (2) that the Christian religion as so set forth requires and is capable of scholarly defence."[9] In his view the battle between liberalism and Christianity had come to a head: "The great redemptive religion which has always been known as Christianity is battling against a totally diverse type of religious belief, which is only the more destructive of the Christian faith because it makes use of traditional Christian terminology." The liberal attempt, as seen in the thought of Shailer Mathews, to reconcile Christian faith and science was wrong "(1) on the ground that it is un-Christian and (2) on the ground that it is unscientific." Although liberals used Christian language, their discussion was not about Christianity; they have "relinquished everything distinctive of Christianity."[10]

Central to Machen's critique was the use of Scripture; here he relied on the "Christian doctrine of inspiration," that the "Bible not only is an account of important things, but that the account itself is true, the writers having been so preserved from error, despite a full maintenance of their habits of thought and expression, that the resulting Book is the 'infallible rule of faith and practice.' " He did not mean a "mechanical" theory of inspiration, that God dictated to "stenographers"; the biblical writers were individuals, using ordinary means for acquiring knowledge, placed in specific historical situations, but "the Holy Spirit so informed the minds of the Biblical writers that they were kept from falling into the errors that mar all other books." For the liberal, the authority of Scripture centered on the "life purpose" of Jesus, but "certain isolated ethical principles of the Sermon on the Mount are accepted, not at all because they are teachings of Jesus, but because they agree with modern ideas." For Machen, "Christianity is founded upon the Bible. . . . Liberalism on the other hand is founded upon the shifting emotions of sinful men." With this use of Scripture liberals picked and chose their way through doctrine, selecting and discarding at will.

Those, for example, who reject the virgin birth of Christ are in essence rejecting the "whole supernatural content of the New Testament, and make of the 'resurrection' just what the word 'resurrection' most emphatically did not mean—a permanence of the influence of Jesus or a mere spiritual existence of Jesus beyond the grave. Old words may here be used, but the thing that they designate is gone."[11]

Fundamentalism came into prominence in the context of this basic debate over the authority of Scripture and the criteria by which theological statements are to be made. The roots of this debate, however, have a longer history.

Historians have interpreted fundamentalism in different though largely complementary ways. Norman Furniss emphasized the conflicts over the interpretation of evolution within Protestant denominations in the period from 1918 to 1931;[12] H. Richard Niebuhr stressed the differences between rural and urban America, commenting, "Fundamentalism in its aggressive forms was most prevalent in those isolated communities in which the traditions of pioneer society had been most effectively preserved and which were least subject to the influence of modern science and industrial civilization."[13] Niebuhr's emphasis was balanced by C. Allyn Russell, who included voices outside rural America.[14] Ernest Sandeen dealt with the intellectual roots of fundamentalism in the nineteenth century, in dispensationalism and Princeton theology, both of which deserve attention.[15]

Through the centuries dispensationalists have argued that the biblical story is an account of the varying ways God's covenant has been made with the human race, a biblical story that is a unified story *and* inerrant. John Nelson Darby (1800–1882), an Anglican priest in Ireland, and Cyrus Ingersoll Scofield (1843–1921), born in Michigan and noted for the Scofield Reference Bible, are two names associated with the movement. Many dispensationalists saw seven periods, closely related to biblical covenants: (1) Innocency, the covenant with

Adam before the Fall; (2) Conscience, the covenant after the Fall; (3) Human Government, the covenant with Noah; (4) the Promise, the covenant with Abraham; (5) the Law, the Mosaic covenant; (6) Grace, the New Covenant in Christ; and (7) the Kingdom, the millennium, when Christ will rule for a thousand years. Under each dispensation different requirements were in effect. With the expectation of the return of Christ and the establishment of the millennium, Sandeen noted, the adherents of dispensationalism espoused a distinctive doctrine of the church. "The church was made up of God's elect who were always only a handful and seldom if ever the possessors of power. The true church could not possibly be identified with any of the large denominations, which were riddled with heresy, but could only be formed by individual Christians who could expect to be saved from the impending destruction."[16] Conferences held during the latter decades of the nineteenth century and the early decades of the twentieth century effectively spread the views of the dispensationalists throughout the country.

Also taking shape in the nineteenth century was the Princeton theology, usually associated with Archibald Alexander, Charles Hodge, and, to some extent, J. Gresham Machen. One of their primary concerns was a doctrine of biblical authority, that God made a self-revelation through an infallible book, that the biblical writings were inerrant and verbally inspired. Sandeen noted that this view of Scripture "became an essential ingredient in the theology of Fundamentalism." These Princeton leaders regarded themselves as rationalists, that the Bible was to be proven to be the Word of God not on the basis of inner testimony but "on the basis of reason through the use of external marks of authenticity."[17] In Sandeen's analysis those influenced by dispensationalism and Princeton theology united against the inroads of modernism. The developing fundamentalist movement thus came out of the North and was not, as Niebuhr had described it, primarily a southern, rural phenomenon.

George Marsden has argued, and persuasively so, that fundamentalism must be interpreted from many angles. At the end of his book *Fundamentalism and American Culture,* he described the movement as a social, political, intellectual, and American phenomenon. In social terms, "Certain key beliefs—inerrancy, anti-evolution, often premillennialism—gained special importance as touchstones to ascertain whether a person belonged to the [fundamentalist] movement. Exactly correct belief then became proportionately more important to the movement as its social basis for cohesiveness decreased." American culture was becoming "less dominated by evangelical values," and common belief became the glue of the movement. In the period after World War I, the threat of godless communism was seen as an ingredient in the conflict between the opposing forces of good and evil. "Satan was assailing Protestant America on every front."[18] It was time to enter the political fray, and the agenda of the fundamentalists became not only theological but also political, as they became concerned about godless public schools, the decay in public morality, and so forth. Intellectually the battle was being joined against the threat of modernism. Fundamentalists insisted that the new sciences, most specifically evolutionary theory, contradicted both true science and common sense. With their vastly different assumptions, the modernist and the fundamentalist simply could not converse with each other.

The Enlightenment and Christian Faith

All of the particular themes described by historians add to our understanding of the sources of the image of purity. In the broadest sense, however, we may view fundamentalism as the conviction that the Enlightenment represented the downfall of Christianity. To support this thesis requires a brief overview of Christian theology since the Reformation.

The patristic, medieval, and Reformation periods presupposed an Aristotelian view of the world. Lay people and theologians lived in a geocentric universe; the earth was the center around which revolved the stars and planets; all was in its place, which God had ordained. That view was presupposed by Paul, Augustine, Pelagius, Aquinas, Luther, and Calvin. When Copernicus wrote *On Celestial Revolutions* in 1543, it was treated by and large as blasphemy; Luther, Calvin, and Roman Catholics were one in condemning it. To say that the earth does not stand still but revolves around the sun contradicted Scripture; Joshua, Scripture reports, commanded the sun to stand still. The psalmist said that the Lord "didst set the earth on its foundations, so that it should never be shaken," (Ps. 104:5). The medieval mind understood the world in just those terms.

The theology of the sixteenth-century reformers presupposed that world view. With the proliferation of debates that soon began among Protestant groups and within particular developing traditions, the lines of doctrinal separation became clearer, yet they all shared a pre-Enlightenment view of the universe. The Augsburg Confession (Lutheran) the Heidelberg Catechism (Calvinist), the Racovian Catechism (Socinian/Unitarian), the Schleiheim Articles (Anabaptist), the Canons and Decrees of the Council of Trent (Roman Catholic), the Synod of Dort (Arminianism), and the Westminster Confession (Puritan/Calvinist) all assumed that world view.

Until the latter part of the seventeenth century, many theological assumptions among Western Christians were the same, despite differences among and within the developing Protestant traditions. Dennis Duling has summarized these beliefs succinctly, all of which were challenged and, for many, undermined by the Enlightenment.

1. Christianity is a revealed religion; that is, the full Christian truth goes beyond what can be

discovered by means of human reason alone. . . .

2. Revelation is based on Scripture and interpreted in the church's teaching as expressed in the creeds of the Ecumenical Councils. . . .

3. Scripture indicates, and the church's teaching defines, the belief that there is a Trinity, one God in three persons—Father, Son, and Holy Spirit.

4. God is the creator who, according to the first chapter in Genesis, created the world out of nothing. The creator is not identical with creation. Yet both God and his created world are good.

5. Adam, the first man, was created with an immortal soul. But Adam sinned and therefore died, and such sin and death have been inherited by the human race (as Original Sin). . . .

6. The Mother of Jesus Christ was a virgin who conceived him miraculously by the Holy Spirit. . . .

7. Jesus Christ is truly God and truly man, two distinct natures in one person, the Mediator between God and humanity, the one who atoned for humanity's sins as the gift of God's grace.

8. Not only was Jesus born miraculously, but his divinity can be proved by his miracles, by his literal fulfillment of prophecy, and by the miracle of his resurrection from the dead and ascension to heaven.

9. Jesus Christ will come again, will be judge of the living and the dead, and will establish his eternal kingdom.

10. Finally, the Bible is a book of revelation to be trusted, including its view that Moses wrote the first five books (the Pentateuch) and that Matthew, Mark, Luke, and John wrote the gospels.[19]

The impact of the newer scientific views shaped a different understanding of one's place in creation. Kepler elaborated on Copernicus's work and argued for an elliptical rather than a circular orbit of the planets and devised a more precise understanding of their velocity; the result was a more developed understanding of the universe in terms of mathematical regularity. Newton in his *Principia* (1687) theorized that the universe was governed by gravitational force and could be understood in terms of the laws of motion. These men were not irreligious, but they were religious in a different sense because their world view was different. To speak of this age as the age of irreligion or this as the time of secularization is to presuppose a particular understanding of religion or even, specifically, Christianity. Peter Gay subtitled a book about the Enlightenment *The Rise of Modern Paganism*. The implication is that a new world view was being born and that the traditional understanding of Christianity was being radically challenged. Yet he wrote: "To speak of the secularization of life in the eighteenth century is not to speak of the collapse of clerical establishments or the decay of religious concerns. The age of the Enlightenment, as the philosophes were among the first to note, was still a religious age; the old association of Christianity and science . . . was shaken in the eighteenth century but not dissolved." To describe this as the age of secularization is "to speak of a subtle shift of attention: religious institutions and religious explanations of events were slowly being displaced from the center of life to its periphery."[20]

Gay's thesis presupposes, however, that a pre-Enlightenment form of Christian theology is the *only* form of Christian theology. That is historically justifiable but not necessarily theologically justifiable. And that is what the even more subtle debate is about. Were the Deists less "religious" than the supporters of the decisions at the Synod of Dort? Did Hume's critique of miracles—"Upon the whole, we may conclude, that the Christian Religion not only was at first attended with miracles, but even at this day cannot be believed by any reasonable person without one"[21]—also presuppose the necessary intertwining of a scholastic world view with the Christian faith? In a vast variety of ways many of the religious thinkers of the Enlightenment were attempting to restate Christian belief in ways that were compatible with the new scientific and philosophical interests of the time. One set of assumptions concerning the structure of the universe led to the rise of "modern paganism"; another set of presuppositions led to an attempt to revitalize the Christian faith. The question became, Is the faith tied to a particular understanding of the universe, or is it not? Does the faith require certain specific beliefs, or are those beliefs, such as the virgin birth of Christ, an infallible Bible, and the historicity of miracles, themselves tied to a world view, so that when the world view collapses, these beliefs also collapse? At what point is the baby thrown out with the bath water? That is the theological question that the Enlightenment raised. How one answers it shows how one views the multitude of new intellectual interests that have shaped our modern world for good or ill.

A recent volume by Harold Lindsell, a contemporary fundamentalist, or moral evangelist, provides a forthright and provocative statement of the issue. In his introduction Lindsell states unambiguously the thesis of his book.

> The Enlightenment will constitute the major consideration of this book. Attention will be given to the major components of the movement that produced a defeat for the church and the virtual end of Western civilization under the rubric of the Judeo-Christian tradition. In place of it we have witnessed the rise of the New Paganism. And the presuppositions of this paganism constitute a new Zeitgeist and Weltanschauung that function as a crucial opponent of historic orthodoxy. Wherever anyone accepts the

> basic views of the Enlightenment, it means the
> end of the Christian faith as we have known it
> through the centuries. All this simply means that
> the tenets of historic orthodoxy are antithetical
> to the tenets of the Enlightenment. To accept
> one standpoint means to deny the other.[22]

Lindsell has been an articulate and prolific spokesperson for our image of purity. He was one of the four founding faculty chosen in May 1947 to lead the newly founded and avowedly conservative Fuller Theological Seminary. A Wheaton College graduate, Lindsell earned a doctoral degree in history from New York University with his primary interest in the relations between the United States and Latin America. After teaching at Columbia (South Carolina) Bible College, he joined the Northern Baptist Seminary in Chicago. From there he was invited to Fuller.[23] In 1968 Lindsell became the editor of *Christianity Today,* a journal founded in 1956 to be a voice for conservative theological concerns and a countervoice to the more liberal *Christian Century.* Through his many articles and books he has been a leader of the fight against modernism and the effects of the Enlightenment.

Lindsell acknowledges his debt to the work of Peter Gay and regrets the lack of attention given to Gay's work and to the themes of the Enlightenment. For Lindsell, the "demise of the church as a primary factor in Western civilization" began during the Enlightenment, a connection that one must understand before realizing the need for a radical change. The founding fathers of the new United States were part and parcel of this debacle. Thomas Jefferson's Deism, for example, led him to devise his own New Testament, devoid of reference to miracles or the supernatural. Although he was instrumental in the founding of the new nation, his lack of Judeo-Christian convictions "was a serious flaw that made possible the decline and fall of the church in our generation." John Adams, nurtured on the writings of the Enlightenment, did not believe that Jesus is God. In Lindsell's understanding, "Christianity has always held that whoever denies the divinity of Jesus Christ is not and cannot be considered a Christian. And whoever is not a Christian is a pagan." Benjamin Franklin, who claimed to be a Deist, was "no supporter of historic orthodoxy and was, like so many others, at best a Christian pagan, which meant that he was no Christian at all."[24]

The effects of the Enlightenment led to nineteenth-century liberalism, and the core of the liberal threat to the Christian faith was biblical criticism. Lindsell cites Ferdinand Christian Baur (1792–1860), David Friedrich Strauss (1808–74), Albrecht Ritschl (1822–89), Julius Wellhausen (1844–1918), and Adolf Harnack (1851–1930) as heirs of the Enlightenment and the leaders of the next generation of destroyers of the faith. Though each of these liberals had a particular interest, they were basically united in their acceptance of biblical criticism; Lindsell implies that biblical critics today continue to follow in their path. Redaction criticism, the form of biblical criticism that investigates how the biblical writers shaped the materials and traditions they received, dominates pagan Christianity.

> Redaction critics begin with the assumption that the writers of the four Gospels were writing theology. In doing this the Gospel writers put into the mouth of Jesus things he never said and attributed to Him acts He never performed. Thus the critics pursue the task of discovering the historical Jesus, that is, the real Jesus, the words He actually spoke, and the acts He really performed. The leaders of this movement have set up a committee whose business it is to determine which of the sayings of Jesus were His and which were redacted back into the Gospels by the writers who used later church traditions. . . . The point at stake, however, is that the critics

are saying that parts of the four Gospels are false. Thus readers are always at a loss to know whether what they read can be trusted. And the pulpiteer must be careful to preface his or her remarks by saying that what is preached about may not be true, leaving listeners perplexed and uncertain about that part of the Word of God. This opens the dike to doubt about all of the Word of God, for the next generation of redaction critics may well destroy the views of its predecessors and emasculate all of the Gospels instead of just parts of them.[25]

Lindsell makes a similar argument concerning the creation story. If Adam and Eve were not "real people," then Jesus, the New Testament writers, and the "great scholars of past ages who all believed in the historicity of Adam and Eve" were wrong. The biblical writings are self-authenticating; "Even a cursory examination of the genealogical tables in the Old and New Testaments witnesses to the historicity of Adam and Eve and of their immediate offspring."[26]

In addition, even theistic evolutionists go contrary to the Word of God in saying that God is the Creator but that "life began with the first atom." In such a view, "science is placed over Scripture and Scripture is relativized and reinterpreted in the light of science's so-called certainties." These theistic evolutionists "have thrown their support to the founding fathers of the Enlightenment." Similarly Marxism is a result of the disregard of biblical authority. "Marxism starts with matter as the ultimate reality, Christianity with God or spirit. Marxism bases its entire world and life view on human reason; Christianity starts with revelation and the supernatural."[27] Liberation theology as an offshoot of Marxism shares its world view, one that is foreign to historic Christianity.

According to Lindsell, all of this change stemming from the Enlightenment has led to the "new Pagan Zeitgeist": the paganization of sex, the breakup of the family, illegitimacy, abortion, homosexuality, pornography, drugs, and the paganization of education; even AIDS can properly be interpreted as the judgment of God. "The New Paganism with its anti-Christian *Weltanschauung* has led to the defeat of the church in the West."[28]

The prophecy that the biblical criticism of the nineteenth and early twentieth centuries would lead to more radical threats to the authority of Scripture has been fulfilled for some in the work of Rudolf Bultmann, whose essay entitled "New Testament and Mythology" precipitated angry debate. His position puts starkly the difference between those who accepted the changes the Enlightenment brought and those who did not. In that seminal essay Bultmann wrote:

> The cosmology of the New Testament is essentially mythical in character. The world is viewed as a three-storied structure with the earth in the centre, the heaven above, and the underworld beneath. Heaven is the abode of God and of celestial beings—the angels. The underworld is hell, the place of torment. Even the earth is more than the scene of natural, everyday events, of the trivial round and common task. It is the scene of the supernatural activity of God and his angels on the one hand, and of Satan and his daemons on the other. These supernatural forces intervene in the course of nature and in all that men think and will and do. Miracles are by no means rare. Man is not in control of his own life. Evil spirits may take possession of him. Satan may inspire him with evil thoughts. Alternatively, God may inspire his thought and guide his purposes. He may grant him heavenly visions. He may allow him to hear his word of succor or demand. He may give him the supernatural power of his Spirit. History does not follow a smooth unbroken course; it is set in motion and controlled by these supernatural

70

powers. This aeon is held in bondage by Satan, sin and death (for "powers" is precisely what they are), and hasten towards its end. That end will come very soon, and will take the form of a cosmic catastrophe. It will be inaugurated by the "woes" of the last time. Then the Judge will come from heaven, the dead will rise, the last judgment will take place, and men will enter into eternal salvation or damnation.

This then is the mythical view of the world which the New Testament presupposes when it presents the event of redemption which is the subject of its preaching. . . .

All this is the language of mythology, and the origin of the various themes can be easily traced in the contemporary mythology of Jewish Apocalyptic and in the redemption myths of Gnosticism. To this extent *the kerygma is incredible to modern man, for he is convinced that the mythical view of the world is obsolete.*[29]

The issue is joined. The heir of the Enlightenment could hear what Bultmann was describing; fundamentalists and many of their conservative brethren, however, argued that such views demolished the authority of Scripture.

If the Bible had not been written in the thought forms and world views of the various writers, then it might be possible to construct a propositional theology that would define clearly the essential and cardinal beliefs of Christians. But it was. Many of the historical doctrines of the Christian faith until the time of the Enlightenment were shared by Christians. No longer, however, do the precise words of doctrinal formulations become transferable to our time without interpretation and reformulation; there are no exceptions. This point, which is

71

obvious to some, is not obvious to all. No creedal statement is in and of itself an essential ingredient of the Christian faith; unless these affirmations are rethought and made our own, they have become theologically dead, although they may serve a strictly liturgical purpose. The image of purity is with us still, in many places and many forms. Where it appears, it may bring fervor and zeal but little that is truly "good news."

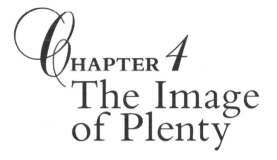

CHAPTER 4
The Image of Plenty

The image of plenty refers not only to the religiously pluralistic character of American society but also to the uncritical tolerance that Americans have for most forms of religious expression. Somehow religion has become a "good thing," especially if it claims the Christian label.

In our public life, generalized religious affirmations surround us. The Supreme Court opens its sessions with a "prayer" to the Almighty: "God save the United States and this Honorable Court." The Senate and House of Representatives do the same and have official chaplains; the armed services have chapels and chaplains; with one exception our presidents have included a reference to God in their inaugural oaths and in their inaugural addresses; our coins and currency mention God; "under God" was put into our Pledge of Allegiance in 1954.

There are historical, constitutional, and national reasons for this preoccupation. To explore it further and to shed light on the image of plenty, this chapter will deal with the formation of the First Amendment and indicate the ways in which that amendment has been interpreted in modern Supreme Court decisions, describe some of the effects of the First Amendment in shaping distinctive characteristics of American religious life, and ask whether the slogan "wall of separation between church and state" is as descriptive or useful as we often and perhaps too easily assume.

The First Amendment and Its Implications

"Congress shall make no law respecting an establishment of religion, or prohibiting the free exercise thereof. . . . " These sixteen words were the result of long, intense debate before they were made part of the First Amendment to the Constitution of the United States. They have continued to confound jurists and justices of the Supreme Court ever since. In the words of Thomas Jefferson they were designed to "erect a wall of separation between Church and State."[1] But the two clauses of the First Amendment—the establishment clause (Congress shall not pass a law establishing religion) and the free-exercise clause (Congress shall not make a law prohibiting the free exercise of religion)—have not been easy to apply. The relation between church and state, or perhaps more properly between "religion" and government, has had a checkered and inconsistent history. Obviously one effect of the First Amendment was to allow American society to become increasingly religiously pluralistic.

Most of the American colonies had a close tie between religious institutions and government, some more elaborate than others. The Massachusetts Bay Colony was established as a commonwealth, with complementary duties for magistrates and clergy. Christian laymen were to govern; ministers were "to exhort" and "attend to Doctrine." The Cambridge Platform of 1648 states: "The powr & authority of Magistrates is not for the restraining of churches, or any other good workes, but for helping in & furthering therof. . . . It is not in the powr of Magistrates to compel their subjects to become church-members, & to partake at the Lords Table." It was as unlawful for church-officers to meddle with the work of the magistrate as it was for church officers to interfere with the magistrate. The roles were defined; the power of the magistrate was not with "things meerly inward, & so not subject to his cognisance & view, as unbeleife [sic], hardness of heart, erronious opinions not vented; but only such things as are acted by the outward man. . . . Idolatry, Blasphemy, Heresy, venting corrupt & pernicious opinions, that destroy the foundation, open contempt of the word preached, prophanation of the Lords day, disturbing the peaceable administration & exercise of the worship & holy things of God, & the like, are to be restrayned, & punished by civil authority."[2] The relation between clergy and magistrate, between the church and civil government, was intimately intertwined yet distinct.

With the passing of time, the children of the first generation and some of the new settlers did not have the fervor of the first generation, and gradually the restriction of voting rights for church members disappeared, as did the requirement for a public testimony of one's regeneration become modified with the Half-Way Covenant of 1662. Both theoretically and practically, however, the tie between the church and the Puritan way of life was close, which may be illustrated by Ola Elizabeth Winslow's description of the meetinghouse as the center of everyday life in early Massachusetts.

> No particular sacredness attached to the building itself. On Sunday the town assembled here for preaching; on town meeting Monday essentially the same group met in the same place to vote "fence repairs," convenient "Horse Bridges," rings for swine, bounty on crows and wolf heads; to specify more trees for the "shade of cattle" or to vote penalties for those who had "deaded" trees contrary to order; to grant one applicant "liberty to set his house upon a Knole," another "liberty" to move into town or to depart; to elect chimney viewers, hog-reaves,

surveyors, constables or other officers, and to
learn "the mind of the town" as to various other
imperatives of their daily lives. . . . The drum-
beat at any other time than the accustomed hour
on Sunday morning was a signal to assemble
here at once for some purpose that brooked no
hesitation. All paths led to this spot of "rising
ground"; all distances to other towns were
measured from the front door.[3]

In such a close-knit community there had to be a tight
knot between the leaders of the church and the civil
officers.

The primary source for Puritans' understanding of
the civil and ecclesiastical realms was Scripture, as it was
in everything else. Perry Miller and Thomas Johnson
have described this reliance on the biblical text as follows:
"The Puritan held that the Bible was sufficiently plain
and explicit so that men with the proper learning, following the proper rules of deduction and interpretation,
could establish its meaning and intention on every subject, not only in theology, but in ethics, costume, di-
plomacy, military tactics, inheritances, profits, mar-
riages, and judicial procedure."[4] But not all in the
colonies agreed on the "proper rules of deduction and
interpretation." From both within and without the New
England churches, voices were raised against the "established" churches.

Anglicans in New England protested the domina-
tion of the Congregational churches; Baptists, historically suspicious of entanglement with the state, became
increasingly restive; immigrants such as Dutch-Reform
Calvinists, German Lutherans, and Scotch-Irish Presbyterians, who had enjoyed majority control in their
homelands, found themselves in a quite different envi-
ronment in the New World and protested the notion of
establishment; individually and together they increasingly sought religious toleration—within, of course, the
broad limits of a presupposed Christian civilization.

The broad themes stemming from the Enlightenment and Pietism contributed to the formation of the First Amendment. Deists and others who accommodated Christian belief to the tests of reason were not hospitable to the power of an established church or clergy. Two examples will suffice. Jefferson, dissatisfied with "orthodox" doctrine, sought to simplify the affirmations of Christians. Not only did he select his own Scripture, but he tried to define the core of the faith itself. In a letter to Benjamin Waterhouse, written in 1822, he said:

> The doctrines of Jesus are simple, and tend all to the happiness of man.
> 1. That there is one only God, and He all perfect.
> 2. That there is a future state of rewards and punishments.
> 3. That to love God with all thy heart and thy neighbor as thyself, is the sum of religion.

These are the great points on which He endeavored to reform the religion of the Jews. But compare with these the demoralizing dogmas of Calvin.

> 1. That there are three Gods.
> 2. That good works, or the love of our neighbor, are nothing.
> 3. That faith is everything, and the more incomprehensible the proposition, the more merit in its faith.
> 4. That reason in religion is of unlawful use.
> 5. That God, from the beginning, elected certain individuals to be saved, and certain others to be damned; and that no crimes of the former can damn them; no virtue of the latter save.[5]

With those assumptions, the disputes over the Trinity and original sin, which had preoccupied much of

New England theology during the eighteenth century, seemed rather inconsequential. Equally suspicious of the theological intricacies of his Presbyterian upbringing, Benjamin Franklin enunciated the common core beliefs of Enlightenment religion.

> I never doubted, for instance, the existence of
> the Deity; that he made the world, and govern'd
> it by Providence; that the most acceptable
> service of God was the doing of good to man;
> that our souls are immortal; and that all crime
> will be punished, and virtues rewarded, either
> here or hereafter. These I esteem'd the essentials
> of every religion; and, being to be found in all
> the religions we had in our country, I respected
> them all, tho' with different degrees of respect,
> as I found them more or less mix'd with other
> articles, which, without any tendency to inspire,
> promote, or confirm morality, serv'd principally
> to divide us, and make us unfriendly to one
> another.[6]

Both Jefferson and Franklin, as children of the Enlightenment, found intolerable the power of the church to control belief.

The Pietist and the heirs of Pietism, for different reasons, also wanted freedom from ecclesiastical control. If the heart of the Pietist understanding of the Christian faith was the heartfelt experience of being regenerated, then there must not be any authority outside the individual to determine the validity of the experience itself; the only judge can be the individual or the community with which one voluntarily associates. The Great Awakenings of the 1730s and 1740s, which affected church life all along the eastern seaboard, enhanced this spirit of voluntarism. Challenges to the settled clergy were made by itinerant clergy; as a result the authority of established churches was undercut. The concerns expressed in Gilbert Tennent's sermon "The Danger of an

Unconverted Ministry" were shared by many of the revivalists of the period of the Great Awakening. Despite differences, however, in the words of Robert Handy, "The goal was much the same—a Christian civilization preparing the way for God's kingdom. It would be realized not through the old way of formal establishments, but by working through those who responded to the outpouring of his spirit."[7] The Great Awakening helped pave the way for democratic sentiments, and it may even be that "what was awakened in 1740 was the spirit of American democracy."[8]

In the debates leading to the formation of the First Amendment, there was no intent to deny the importance of religious convictions in the fundamental structure of the new nation, though there was fear of any national established church. Only in Article 6 of the United States Constitution, which prohibited religious tests for national office, was the word *religion* used, yet common religious assumptions, largely derived from Enlightenment Christianity, were important. The frequently quoted words of James Madison in his "Memorial and Remonstrance on the Religious Rights of Man" give clear expression of his Enlightenment sentiments and sum up the attitude of many.

> Because we hold it for a "fundamental and undeniable truth," that religion, or the duty we owe to our creator, and the manner of discharging it, can be directed only by reason and conviction, not by force or violence. The religion, then, of every man, must be left to the conviction and conscience of every man; and it is the right of every man to exercise it as these may dictate. This right is, in its nature, an unalienable right. It is unalienable, because the opinions of men, depending only on the evidence contemplated in their own minds, cannot follow the dictates of other men; it is unalienable, also, because what is here a right

towards men, is a duty towards the creator. It is
the duty of every man to render the creator such
homage, and *such only*, as he believes to be
acceptable to him; this duty is precedent, both in
order of time and degree of obligation, to the
claims of civil society. Before any man can be
considered as a member of civil society, he must
be considered as a subject of the governor of the
universe; and if a member of civil society, who
enters into any subordinate association, must
always do it with a reservation of his duty to the
general authority, much more must every man
who becomes a member of any particular civil
society do it *with the saving his allegiance to the
universal sovereign.*[9]

For there to be a *United* States there must be some
commonly shared religious convictions. Consider here
some of the wordings proposed during the debates in
1789, and ultimately rejected, for the article on religion
in the Bill of Rights.

The Civil Rights of none shall be abridged on
account of religious belief or worship, nor shall
any national religion be established, nor shall the
full and equal rights of conscience be in any
manner, nor on any pretext infringed.

No religion shall be established by law, nor shall
the equal rights of conscience be infringed.

Congress shall make no law establishing religion, or to prevent the free exercise thereof, or
to infringe the rights of conscience.

Congress shall make no law establishing one
religious sect or society in preference to others,
or to infringe on the rights of conscience.

Congress shall not make any law infringing the
rights of conscience, or establishing any religious
sect or society.

Congress shall make no law establishing any
particular denomination of religion in preference
to another, or prohibiting the free exercise
thereof, nor shall the rights of conscience be
infringed.

Congress shall make no law establishing religion, or prohibiting the free exercise thereof.

Congress shall make no law establishing articles
of faith or a mode of worship, or prohibiting
the free exercise of religion.[10]

Even the choice of *an* in the text ("Congress shall
make no law respecting *an* establishment of religion,
. . .") had its significance. In the argument of Michael
Malpin, the wording "an establishment" rather than "the
establishment" was chosen to ensure "the legality of
nondiscriminatory aid. . . . They were showing that
they wanted to prohibit only those official activities that
tended to promote the interests of one or another particular sect."[11]

The Growth of Denominationalism

With the enactment of the First Amendment the
themes noted by the foreign travelers became dominant
characteristics of mainline Protestantism in America:
persuasion, not coercion, as the method of winning
members; voluntarism as the structure of ecclesiastical
institutions; revivalism as the tool; and a tendency to
minimize theological doctrine and stress morality as the
identifying characteristic of the Christian life.

One example of the new emphases can be seen in
the work of the itinerant Methodist revivalist Peter Cartwright (1785–1872). Like many others, Cartwright conducted missionary tours with a copy of Scripture as his
only companion; nothing more was needed. In his autobiography he wrote about a tour he had made through
the Cumberland Mountains.

I journeyed on toward my home in Christian county, Kentucky. Saturday night came on, and found me in a strange region of country, and in the hills, knobs, and spurs of Cumberland Mountains. I greatly desired to stop on the approaching Sabbath, and spend it with a Christian people; but I was now in a region of country where there was no Gospel minister for many miles around, and where, as I learned, many of the scattered population had never heard a Gospel sermon in all their lives, and where the inhabitants knew no Sabbath only to hunt and visit, drink and dance. Thus lonesome and pensive, late in the evening, I hailed at a tolerably-decent house, and the landlord kept entertainment. I rode up and asked for quarters. The gentleman said I could stay, but he was afraid I would not enjoy myself very much as a traveler, inasmuch as they had a party meeting there that night to have a little dance. I inquired how far it was to a decent house of entertainment on the road; he said seven miles. I told him if he would treat me civilly and feed my horse well, by his leave I would stay. He assured me I should be treated civilly. I dismounted and went in. The people collected, a large company. I saw there was not much drinking going on.

I quietly took my seat in one corner of the house, and the dance commenced. I sat quietly musing, a total stranger, and greatly desired to preach to this people. Finally, I concluded to spend the next day—Sabbath—there, and ask the privilege to preach to them. I had hardly settled this point in my mind, when a beautiful, ruddy young lady walked very gracefully up to me, dropped a handsome courtesy, and pleasantly, with winning smiles, invited me out to take a dance with her. I can hardly describe my thoughts or feelings on that occasion. However,

in a moment I resolved on a desperate experiment. I rose as gracefully as I could; I will not
say with some emotion, but with many
emotions. The young lady moved to my right
side; I grasped her right hand with my right
hand, while she leaned her left arm on mine. In
this position we walked on the floor. The whole
company seemed pleased at this act of politeness
in the young lady, shown to a stranger. . . . I
then spoke to the fiddler to hold a moment, and
added that for several years I had not undertaken
any matter of importance without first asking
the blessing of God upon it, and I desired now
to ask the blessing of God upon this beautiful
young lady and the whole company, that had
shown such an act of politeness to a total
stranger.

Here I grasped the young lady's hand
tightly, and said, "Let us all kneel down and
pray," and then instantly dropped on my knees,
and commenced to praying with all the power
of soul and body that I could command. The
young lady tried to get loose from me, but I
held her tight. Presently she fell on her knees.
Some of the company kneeled, some stood,
some fled, some sat still, all looked curious. . . .

While I prayed some wept, and wept out
aloud, and some cried for mercy. I rose from
my knees and commenced an exhortation, after
which I sang a hymn. The young lady who
invited me on the floor lay prostrate, crying
earnestly for mercy. I exhorted again, I sang and
prayed nearly all night. About fifteen of that
company professed religion, and our meeting
lasted next day and next night, and as many
more were powerfully converted. I organized a
society, took thirty-two into the Church, and
sent them a preacher.[12]

In this way, another Methodist church began. Such a story illustrates the principle and power of voluntarism at work.

Between 1780 and 1860, the Baptists and the Methodists showed spectacular growth in the United States. Together, they have had a tremendous influence in the shaping of American religious life. In 1780 there were 457 Baptist congregations; in 1820, 2,700; and in 1860, 12,150. Methodist churches grew even faster, from 2,700 in 1820 to 19,883 in 1860. In sharp contrast, Congregationalists went from 749 in 1780 to only 1,100 in 1820 and 2,234 in 1860; Anglicans, from 406 in 1780 to only 600 in 1820 and 2,145 in 1860.[13]

At the beginning of the nineteenth century it is estimated that approximately one out of ten Americans was a member of a religious body. As the nineteenth century progressed, however, standards for church membership declined or became less stringent, pluralism took root, and toleration gradually became acceptable.[14] America was becoming a religiously pluralistic society.

Supreme Court Interpretations of the First Amendment

In recent decades the fact of religious pluralism has caused difficulty for the Supreme Court in interpreting how the First Amendment is to be applied. A brief look at some important cases since the 1940s will illustrate the legal implications of pluralism.

The large influx of Catholic immigrants in the nineteenth and early twentieth centuries changed the character of American religious life. This caused periodic waves of unreasoned hostility by Protestants to the growth of what some called "popery." It also caused conflict among Roman Catholics; some wanted to adapt characteristics of Protestant churches, for example, in a greater role for laity, the use of revivalistic measures, and the need to identify an American Catholic experience. The public school system, an important creation of the nineteenth century, was dominated by a Protestant mentality, and Roman Catholics objected to the use in the schools of the King James Version of the Bible, a "Protestant" Bible, and different from their canonical version of Scripture. For this and other obvious reasons the parochial school system developed, to which Catholics could send their children, at their expense, for primary and secondary education. Catholics were taxed for the support of the public school and also contributed to the maintenance of their own institutions.

In *Everson v. Board of Education* (1947) the Supreme Court dealt with a New Jersey statute that granted reimbursement to parents of Roman Catholic children for public transportation to their parochial school. Does the First Amendment permit such reimbursement? In a 5-4 decision the Court ruled that the law did not violate the Constitution, because, in the words of Justice Black, who wrote the majority opinion, "the First Amendment has erected a wall between church and state. That wall must be kept high and impregnable. We could not approve the slightest breach. New Jersey has not breached it here." The core of his argument was that since New Jersey paid the fare of children going to public schools, there is no constitutional reason why it should not also reimburse Catholic parents. The transportation was serving a secular purpose (namely, education), and therefore the state could not discriminate against Catholic children on the basis of their religious convictions. His argument was based on the establishment clause.

> The "establishment of religion" clause of the First Amendment means at least this: Neither a state nor the Federal Government can set up a church. Neither can pass laws which aid one religion, aid all religions, or prefer one religion over another. Neither can force nor influence a person to go to or to remain away from church

against his will or force him to profess a belief
or disbelief in any religion. No person can be
punished for entertaining or professing religious
beliefs or disbeliefs, for church attendance or
non-attendance. No tax in any amount, large or
small, can be levied to support any religious
activities or institutions, whatever they may be
called, or whatever form they may adopt to
teach or practice religion. Neither a state nor the
Federal Government can, openly or secretly,
participate in the affairs of any religious organizations or groups and vice versa. In the words
of Jefferson, the clause against establishment of
religion by law was intended to erect a "wall of
separation between Church and State."[15]

In his dissent, Justice Rutledge, citing Madison's "Memorial and Remonstrance," argued that the majority
decision was a violation of the First Amendment. "The
funds used here were raised by taxation. . . . It aids them
[the children] in a substantial way to get the very thing
which they are sent to the particular school to secure,
namely, religious training and teaching."[16] (Justice
Douglas, who voted with the majority, wrote in 1962,
in *Engle v. Vitale,* that the majority decision here was
wrongly decided.) This case illustrates the difficulty of
applying the establishment and the free-exercise clauses
of the First Amendment in an increasingly pluralistic
culture.

Another important decision was reached in *Zorach
v. Clauson* (1952). In 1948 the Court had ruled 8-1 in
McCollum v. Board of Education that provision for classes
in religious instruction for public school children on
public school premises during school hours was uncon-
stitutional. In 1952 the issue was whether or not it was
constitutional for children to be released during school
hours to attend religious instruction programs off public
school premises; the Court ruled, 6-3, that this did not
violate the First Amendment. In writing the majority

opinion, Justice Douglas stated: "We are a religious people whose institutions presuppose a Supreme Being. We guarantee the freedom to worship as one chooses. . . . When the state encourages religious instruction or co-operates with religious authorities by adjusting the schedule of public events to sectarian needs, it follows the best of our traditions. For it then respects the religious nature of our people and accommodates the public service to their spiritual needs." In dissent, Justice Black argued, "This [practice] is beyond all question a utilization of the tax established and tax supported public school system to aid religious groups to spread their faiths. And it falls squarely under the ban of the First Amendment."[17] Bus transportation, to Black, did not violate the First Amendment because it served a secular purpose; released time for religious instruction off public school grounds, however, was in his view a violation. Justice Jackson concluded in his opinion in *McCollum v. Board of Education* that Jefferson's "wall between church and state" may become "as winding as the famous serpentine wall designed by Mr. Jefferson" for his beloved University of Virginia,[18] a prophecy that began to be fulfilled in *Zorach v. Clauson.*

Three other important cases dealt with aspects of religious pluralism: *Braunfeld v. Braun* (1961), *Sherbert v. Verner* (1963), and *Wisconsin v. Yoder* (1972). In *Braunfeld v. Braun* the issue was whether or not an Orthodox Jew must close his place of business on Sunday, even though he is obligated under Jewish custom to close his business in observance of the Sabbath, or Saturday. The majority of the court ruled that the Christian Sabbath, though it had a religious origin, had become a day for "rest, relaxation and family togetherness"; the state was therefore within its rights to enact Sunday blue laws. In *Sherbert v. Verner* the decision of the state of South Carolina to deny unemployment benefits to a Seventh-Day Adventist who refused to work on Saturday, her Sabbath, and who lost her job was a violation of her rights under the First Amendment. In *Wisconsin v. Yoder* the issue concerned the compulsory school attendance law in Wisconsin. Members of the Conservative Amish Mennonite Church refused to send their children to public school after they had graduated from the eighth grade because this was contrary to their religious conviction that such education would endanger their own salvation and that of their children. The majority opinion of the Court said that because of the long history of the Amish as a "successful and self-sufficient segment of American society . . . and the vital role that belief and daily conduct play in the continued survival of the Old Order Amish communities and religious organization," their rights under the First Amendment would be violated if they were forced to continue in public school beyond the eighth grade.[19] Clearly these issues were not considered when the First Amendment was formed.

The decision in *Engle v. Vitale* (1962) caused a national uproar still with us today. The regents of the state of New York had devised the following prayer for use in the School District of New Hyde Park: "Almighty God, we acknowledge our dependence upon Thee, and we beg Thy blessings upon us, our parents, our teachers and our Country." The use of this nondenominational and rather innocuous prayer was challenged, and the Court ruled 8-1 that the use of the prayer was a violation of the First Amendment. In his concurring affirmative decision Justice Douglas wrote: "The First Amendment leaves the Government in a position not of hostility to religion but of neutrality. The philosophy is that the atheist or agnostic—the nonbeliever—is entitled to go his own way. The philosophy is that if government interferes in matters spiritual, it will be a divisive force." In his lone dissent Justice Stewart argued, "I think that to deny the wish of these school children to join in reciting this prayer is to deny them the opportunity of sharing in the spiritual heritage of our Nation."[20] The *Engle v. Vitale* ruling convinced many that the United States was becoming a godless land, separated from its religious roots.

This brief survey of important Court cases indicates the difficult legal implications of our increasingly pluralistic society and the seemingly inconsistent way in which the First Amendment has been applied and no doubt will continue to be applied. The majority decision written by Justice Burger in *Lemon v. Kurtzman* (1971) set out guidelines to be used. This case concerned legislation passed in Rhode Island and Pennsylvania that permitted tax monies to be used for reimbursement for teachers in nonpublic schools (Rhode Island) and reimbursement for teacher salaries, textbooks, and instructional materials used in nonpublic schools (Pennsylvania). The court held that such laws were a violation of the First Amendment. In his decision Justice Burger offered the following guidelines to constitutionality: "First, the statute must have a secular legislative purpose; second, its principal or primary effect must be one that neither advances nor inhibits religion; finally, the statute must not foster 'an excessive entanglement with religion.' "[21] Those guidelines do not solve the problem, but they indicate how exceedingly difficult it is to unravel the relation of religion and government in our society and indicate that there may be even more subtle factors at work. Justice Douglas hinted at one of them in his opinion in the *Zorach* case when he wrote, "We are a religious people whose institutions presuppose a Supreme Being."

The unstated ingredient in the decisions of the Supreme Court was, perhaps, best stated by Chief Justice Charles Evans Hughes in a comment to William O. Douglas. "Justice Douglas you must remember one thing. At the constitutional level where we work, ninety percent of any decision is emotional. The rational part of us supplies the reasons for supporting our predilections."[22]

American Civil Religion

In chapter 1 Francis Grund was quoted as saying: "Religion has been the basis of the most important

American settlements; religion kept their little community together—religion assisted them in their revolutionary struggles. . . . The Americans look upon religion as a promoter of civil and political liberty." He
noted also the link between religion and morality. "The
deference which the Americans pay to morality is scarcely inferior to their regard for religion. . . . They see in
a breach of morals a direct violation of religion; and in
this, an attempt to subvert the political institutions of
the country." Grund and other foreign visitors were perceptive in noting what in the 1960s came to be called
American "civil religion," a label given currency in an
article published in 1967 by Robert Bellah. Bellah remarked, "Civil religion at its best is a genuine appre-
hension of universal and transcendent religious reality
as seen in or, one could almost say, as revealed through
the experience of the American people."[23]

    This civil religion has Jewish and Christian roots;
and events in American history have been given a rev-
elatory character; the *"immediate events of revelation [are]
events in the American experience,"* such as the American
Revolution and the Civil War.

> The first was a moment when God delivered the
> colonies from Pharaoh Britain and the "evils" of
> the Old World, revealed the purposes of the
> nation, and adopted the Young Republic as an
> example and instrument of freedom and repub-
> lican government for the rest of the world. The
> Civil War was the nation's first real "time of
> testing" when God tried the permanence of the
> Union or, in some interpretations, brought
> judgment upon his wayward people. Documents
> like the Declaration of Independence and the
> Gettysburg Address function as scriptures that
> interpret these events and hence preserve the
> traditions of the civil religion. Washington
> becomes both Moses and Joshua, both the deliv-
> erer of the American people out of bondage and

the leader of the chosen people into the Prom-
ised Land of independence. Lincoln assumes the
role of a Christ figure in the national memory:
one who tragically dedicated himself to the
destiny of a united nation and whose death
summed up the sacrifices that redeemed the
nation for that destiny.[24]

Similarly, Memorial Day became a day of religious observance.[25] This horizontal, common-denominator civil
religion has been vehemently attacked by those who find
this to be a corruption of traditional affirmations, or
what may be called "vertical" religion.

The high point of religious affiliation in America
was reached in 1958, when 63.4 percent of the population
said they belonged to a religious group. Will Herberg,
writing out of the tradition of Conservative Judaism,
was highly critical of this surge of piety,[26] a critique
influenced by the work of Marcus Hansen on American
immigration.[27] Herberg interpreted American religious
history as the process of assimilating successive generations of immigrants. The first generation sought to
retain its identity through retention of language, custom,
and religion. The second generation attempted to become Americanized in language and practices and religious traditions and, as a result, became less differen-
tiated. The third generation sought identity by seeking
to reclaim their general religious traditions and identified
themselves as Protestant, Catholic, or Jew, yet without
the particularism of these traditions. These tendencies,
in part, account for the surge of piety in the 1950s.

Herberg quoted Dwight Eisenhower, who con-
fessed: "I am the most intensely religious man I know.
Nobody goes through six years of war without faith.
That does not mean that I adhere to any sect. A democracy cannot exist without a religious base. I believe
in democracy."[28] Such sentiments are very much like
those some of the foreign travelers observed in America

in the early and middle nineteenth century. What Herberg observed was not as new as he claimed. Rather, in our history we have had a tradition of Enlightenment religion, with its commonly shared, theologically innocuous religious beliefs (such as those professed by James Madison), which have existed alongside the vertical, denominationally self-conscious traditions.

Sidney Mead has made a very important analysis of these two strands. He asks, Are the two theologies reconcilable; and if so, how; and if not, which is to be chosen? By the two theologies he means (1) the Enlightenment form of religious expression, which has been offered by Jefferson and Madison, in civil religion, in Justice Douglas's comment in the *Zorach* case, and in the perspective represented by the affirmation of Dwight Eisenhower; and (2) the particularistic, self-conscious affirmations of belief as seen in confessional patterns of the nineteenth century, for example, those of John Nevin, and Princeton theology and more recently in the theological concerns underlying the interpretations of Will Herberg, Martin Marty, and others. (When they speak on political issues, the fundamentalists describe our age as a time of godlessness because of *Engle v. Vitale, Roe v. Wade,* pornography, homosexuality, the divided family, and so forth, but they are careful when addressing a general audience to minimize their particularistic theological views.) Those who are critical of civil religion, of American piety, who call for a recovery of religious particularity and are pained by politicians who say "America is great because she is good," make us wonder whose "particularity" they want to recapture "from the pluralistic grab bag—whether that of John Cotton, or of Roger Williams, of Issac Backus or of Timothy Dwight, or of C. F. W. Walther or of Samuel S. Schmucker, of Reinhold Niebuhr or of Carl McIntyre. Mead adds, "Church members in America have always been faced with the necessity to choose, implicitly at least, between the inclusive religion of democracy and the particularistic Christianity of their sect."[29]

Given our increasing religious pluralism (the variety of options of religious commitment are greater today than they ever have been), we are presented with an even more confusing choice today; no longer is it simply a choice between the religion of democracy or civil religion over against particularistic theologies. Rather, different understandings of civil religion vie with religiously particularistic options that have outgrown the borders of the Jewish-Christian traditions, for now we have, among others, black theology, liberation theology, and feminist theology, which do not have institutional form but thrive both within and without organized traditions. In addition, religious movements, many of which have non-Western roots, have attracted wide attention: Hare Krishna, Zen Buddhism, the Unification Church and even more alternatives are available in the flourishing self-help groups.[30]

In the nineteenth century the foreign traveler in the United States was struck by the variety of Christian groups and their distinctive and common characteristics. If Francis Grund and Alexis de Tocqueville were to return today, they would probably be initially bewildered by what they saw but upon reflection would not be surprised. Yet the religious pluralism of the 1990s is certainly much different than it was in 1890 or 1820. The deference Americans pay to religion today is probably no different, although now, one may argue, it is much more difficult to describe what a Christian is.

Tolerance is not necessarily a virtue. In our history we have been confronted with a wide variety of religious bodies, many claiming the label *Christian*. Under our Constitution all have that right. In the process, however, we lose sight of any relation to the roots of the tradition itself. No one would suggest reinstituting the Inquisition, but certainly those who claim an allegiance to a tradition must somehow learn to state what that allegiance is. This we have not done very successfully, and yet it is something we must begin to do—not to separate one from another but to find the basis for meaningful and creative dialogue. The analogy of this nation as a melting pot affirms that those from different nationalities, creeds, and races have the still-unrealized possibility of equal opportunity, but it can also lead to a blandness and too-easy tolerance that boils away the vitality and creative energy that can come from a consciousness of our differences as well as our similarities.

CHAPTER 5
Re-Imaging Protestantism in America

Each age must find its own way to conceive of the thrust of the Christian faith. In this book I have suggested images of faith through which American Protestants have sought to forge a distinctive Christian identity that made sense of their doctrinal traditions, their moral mandates, and their engagement in the American experiment. These extremely influential notions functioned as symbols of religious integrity and as ideals that fueled and guided the many and varied creative religious endeavors of Protestantism in America.

Yet piety, purity, and plenty should no longer be the dominant images of religious authenticity. The disenchantment and alienation that many people today experience are clues to their conceptual inadequacy. In this chapter we probe behind the images to their root in the Christian notion of redemption. We look to an often-neglected element in Christian thought about redemption—its corporate dimension—and we offer that image of corporate atonement as one that might challenge and stimulate American Protestantism to a deeper engagement with itself and with the exigencies of our contemporary world.

Inadequacies of the Images

The Christian faith, as we have seen, has often been viewed with the assumption that "religion" is in some fashion a good thing, apart from the content of what is believed, and that different expressions of the Christian faith carry equal validity. That is the image of plenty. The religiously pluralistic character of our history has encouraged a mood of toleration, almost for toleration's sake. As Americans, we are a so-called melting pot, a collection of different nationalities and religious backgrounds. In fact we have hundreds of different religious groups in contemporary American society, many of which are not Christian and many of which are indigenous. The foreign travelers were continually impressed with or amazed at our religious diversity and even the diversity within mainline traditions themselves.

Somewhere in the process, however, we have lost a habit of critical assessment or, perhaps more specifically, the willingness to ask what in all of this is Christian. Do all "Christian" groups have the same justification to claim the label? Certainly the answer to that question is theological and not simply historical. Not all religions are the same; nor are all Christians who claim the label talking about the same thing. The devout dedication of a Jerry Falwell or a Peter Cartwright or a William Jennings Bryan does not necessarily a Christian make. So while the pluralistic character of our society is culturally a decided plus, a model to be treasured, it also encourages a willingness to allow anyone to claim a religious label, whether appropriate and justifiable or not. The image of plenty leaves unresolved the question of what is normatively Christian.

Second, some people insist that a Christian is one who believes certain specific, identifiable items of faith. That is the image of purity. To make that claim, however, is to hold unexamined presuppositions about the Christian faith that are, I believe, untenable in our age. The doctrine of the Trinity, for example, might be said to have biblical roots and therefore be essential to Christian faith. But certainly its formulation in the Nicene Creed (325 C.E.) employs language that is not biblical. Creeds have developed not so much as expressions of uncontested faith but as means for setting limits on what counts as "right belief," or orthodoxy.

For many centuries, for example, the Apostles' Creed was thought to have been written by the twelve apostles, each one writing a sentence. But we now know that its core was written in the second century to rule out certain positions in the theologically amorphous Christian world. Many who claimed allegiance to the church held, for example, that the God of the Hebrews was an evil creator God. The true, hidden God of mercy and love was revealed only in Jesus Christ; this God had no relation to the biblical account of what the Christians later called the Old Testament. Moreover, for this faction Jesus Christ did not have a full, concrete human existence; his body was an illusion (docetism). In part, therefore, the confession that later developed into the Apostles' Creed was formulated to rule out this Marcionite, or two-God, affirmation. Gradually a consensus was reached that the biblical God is one: "I believe in God, the all-sovereign father" (that is, sovereign over all creation and the creator of all that is) "and in Jesus Christ, His Son" (that is, the Son of the creator God); "Who was born, died and was buried" (that is, he had a concrete human existence and was not a phantom). Perhaps one can infer from this statement that God is triune, but nowhere does it so state.

Formation of the Nicene Creed was even more complex; it involved weighty philosophical issues as well as deeply held religious concerns. Deliberations at the Council of Nicea, summoned by Emperor Constantine, fastened on to the phrase "of one substance with the Father" to describe Jesus Christ. They thereby ruled out those Christians who were saying that Christ was neither fully God nor fully man. In concluding that God the

Father and God the Son were of the same status, co-eternal, the council was clearly on the road to the doctrine of the Trinity. The bulk of its creed therefore describes the relation of the Son to the Father. Only the short opening paragraph deals with God the Father, and the short concluding paragraph merely mentions, "I believe in the Holy Spirit."

My point is while doctrinal issues enjoined by the ancient creeds are significant and important, the credal solutions are in language not easily translatable either back into biblical language or into the twentieth-century idiom. Therefore the specific Nicene formulation of the doctrine of the Trinity cannot be made a sine qua non of Christian belief. Those who hold that the Christian faith simply demands assent to some catalog of five or seven or twenty propositions have not read their history carefully. They are making theological demands that fly in the face of historical evidence, even though one can argue that many Christians have nearly always insisted on certain propositional affirmations. The summary of Christian belief that was quoted in chapter 3, for example, which concerned beliefs of Christians at the beginning of the Enlightenment, is just and reliable; and some people who claim the label *Christian* would hold to these affirmations today. Moreover, historically those affirmations did serve to unite or at least to define Christians. But the assumptions that undergird them, cosmologically and theologically, are now rightfully challenged. Those purists who argue that the Christian faith is a doctrinal monolith are themselves simply adding their faith-claim to a long and variegated list of Christian faith-claims. The image of purity is inadequate for facing or overcoming the incontrovertible historical fact of doctrinal pluralism.

Third, for many the image of piety shapes their view of the Christian faith. I defined the image of piety in chapter 2 as an unreflective and uncritical acceptance of moral precepts that are clothed in Christian language and demand heartfelt response and defense. This has been

98

a powerful theme in American religious history. Yet its assumption is that the Christian life is well defined, biblically traceable, and obvious. In recent years much attention has been given to the moral evangelists, particularly to Jerry Falwell, Jimmy Swaggart, and other televangelists. From them and others we have heard about the decay of morality in high government offices, in boards of corporations, in nominees for public office, in ghetto life—simply everywhere. Falwell has even commented that if God does not punish America soon, he must apologize to Sodom and Gomorrah. The moral evangelists not only "know" what is wrong with contemporary society, they also make the assumption that simply by being "born again," one will know what is the Christian thing to do. But how do we know what that is? If we had prayer in public schools, if homosexuality were recognized as aberrant behavior and a sin, if healthy family togetherness were restored, if America's role as a moral Christian nation were recaptured, if people would only work harder and recognize the virtues of capitalism and the godlessness of communism—if all these, then somehow would the world be turned around?

But the underpinnings of the theme of piety have produced an image that may have little to do with Christian faith itself. No one has yet identified the supposed Golden Age to which we American Christians must return. Was it in the Great Depression, in the Civil War, on the frontier, or in the Puritan wilderness? The further assumption that the Gospels lay out rules and regulations for the Christian life and that the magically pristine biblical period is the norm reads history through rose-colored glasses. Those who see Christianity in these terms are unwilling to live with ambiguity in any form, or want somehow to recapture the good, the true, and the beautiful from a Christian age that never was.

This characterization of the Christian faith also rests on a view of human nature that assumes that humans are capable of achieving sinless behavior if only they will to do so. Despite the moral evangelists' appeal to the

sin in us all, their view of human nature manifests an
unadulterated Pelagianism. The sin with which they are
concerned is behavior, and there is no shred of evidence
that the human being today is less or more morally pure
than at some earlier stage in our Christian history. Their
idealized past exists only in the imagination.

My conviction is that the infidel misses the point
as much as does Jerry Falwell, that Peter Cartwright is
no closer to the truth than Russell Conwell or those who
insist America is great because she is good. Rather, the
Christian faith leaves us with no ready answers or easy
path. It does not offer an unambiguous life in which
issues and answers are clear cut. The image of moral
piety fails to meet the complexities and ambiguities of
moral life today. To say this, however, does not imply
that the Christian faith leaves us in a morass of indecision,
without conviction or program. Definitive answers may
be elusive, but our assumptions must be rethought.

Traditional Views of the Atonement

In seeking an image of Christian identity adequate
to contemporary life and consonant with Christian tradition, we must look to a fundamental Christian notion:
the atonement. Christianity arose in a time of apocalyptic
expectation, when many assumed that the end of the
world was at hand. In Jesus of Nazareth some saw the
Christ, the messiah. Although some saw this Jesus as
part of the lineage of the Hebrew prophets, the gathered
community, the church, saw in him not merely another
prophetic teacher but the fulfillment of Hebrew prophecy. The church saw him as redeemer, and Christianity
was a religion of redemption. God was in Christ, reconciling the world to Godself. But what is the nature
of this redemption?

Christian theologians have long said that human
redemption is brought about by the atoning work of
Jesus Christ, although there have been many different

interpretations of how that atoning work is accomplished. A brief review of three of these classical theories may help bring into focus the problems this doctrine has presented.

More than other statements of the "work" of Christ, the so-called classical theory of St. Anselm (1033–1109) has been at the center of many theological systems. His formulation of the "satisfaction" theory is contained in his *Cur Deus Homo* (Why God-Man?).[1] The essay consists of two parts. The first deals with the unbeliever's critique of Christianity; the second argues that without the God-man, Christ, redemption cannot be obtained. The dialogue form of the essay provides a convenient means for Anselm to state his position. Through his naive questioner, Boso, he was able to pose many of the traditional problems and positions. Anselm sought to show that satisfaction, or recompense, is paid to God in the atoning work of the God-man and not to the devil, as the "ransom to the devil" theory had been stated by Gregory I (d. 604). Humanity deserves to be punished; its sin is an infinite sin because it is a sin against God. Humanity owes all it has and can do to God. But God's justice also needs to be satisfied, and this humanity cannot achieve. Salvation can come only through one who is both God, able to offer commensurate satisfaction, and man, responsible for the debt.

Anselm's thesis concerning satisfaction reflects the concepts of sovereignty and justice in feudal society. Sin is essentially rebellion against the sovereign Lord, a refusal of one to render his or her all to God. The King of the universe, like the king of an earthly realm, demands justice and satisfaction for the injury done to his creation. That is the plight of humanity. Anselm offers one interpretation of the restoration of humanity's relationship with God.

Abelard (1079–1142) has been a figure of controversy in the history of Christian thought. The story of his love affair with Héloise, his theological battles with other medieval scholastics, and his condemnation by the

83621

Synod of Soissons in 1121 has been told and frequently romanticized. Abelard's theory of the atonement, sharply contrasting with Anselm's "satisfaction" theory or the older "ransom to the devil" interpretation, was developed in his *Exposition of the Epistle to the Romans*. His thesis has frequently been called the "moral influence theory," a label open to misinterpretation. The term *moral* tends to obscure the decidedly Christian element in his position. Abelard insisted that the work of Christ was to demonstrate the need for human response to the grace of God shown in Christ.

> Now it seems to us that we have been justified
> by the blood of Christ and reconciled to God in
> this way: through this unique act of grace mani-
> fested to us—in that his Son has taken upon
> himself our nature and persevered therein in
> teaching us by word and example even unto
> death—he has more fully bound us to himself by
> love; with the result that our hearts should be
> enkindled by such a gift of divine grace, and
> true charity should not now shrink from
> enduring anything for him.[2]

Here the emphasis is not so much on satisfaction of the justice of God as it is on the response initiated in the human being.

Hugo Grotius (1583–1645) was a Dutch historian, political theorist, and theologian. Though he is remembered most frequently for his *de Jure Belli et Pacis* (On the law of war and peace; 1624), a major work in political theory, he was also involved in the Arminian controversy in the Dutch Reformed Church. His defense of the Arminian position and protest against the secular interference in religious affairs caused his imprisonment and later exile from the Netherlands. His doctrine of the atonement, usually referred to as the "governmental" theory, was developed in reaction to the Socinian position. In contrast to these sixteenth-century "Unitarians" (who viewed the work of Christ as an example for

102

humankind that commands an obedient response) and to the "satisfaction" theory of Anselm (which suggested that Christ satisfied the human debt to God), Grotius proposed that the work of Christ was to uphold divine law and government. God is the legal governor of the universe, the administrator of law, but in the death of Christ God displayed God's clemency, hatred of sin, and insistence on the authority of divine law. The punishment due humans for their sin could not be ignored. And even though God did not demand satisfaction, God's law must be preserved. This was the work of Christ. Grotius's "governmental" theory had marked influence on Calvinism, especially in eighteenth-century America.

Each of these theories presents problems for dealing with the character of sin. Anselm's position, which has been so influential in the history of Christian theology, is tied to feudal imagery that has little meaning today. And Anselm actually dealt more with a christological issue than with a soteriological one. Abelard's thesis presents problems if the radical nature of sin in human life is taken seriously; it is certainly much more agreeable to a pietistic understanding of the nature of the Christian faith. The governmental theory of Grotius, like that of Anselm, is tied to a world view that many no longer share. What choices are left?

Sin and the Community

If Christianity is to be understood as the redemptive activity of God, from what is one being redeemed? Christians have assumed that there is a universal human predicament for which Christian faith has a relevant answer. According to Genesis 1, humans were created in the image of God. That is, the human ability to know God differentiates him or her from other aspects of the created order. Genesis 2 contains the account of Adam and Eve and the disruption that comes into an order that was created good. The point of that story may be interpreted, not that Adam and Eve disobeyed a command, but that they, created with the potential to know God, sought instead to possess the knowledge that God has. In this interpretation sin is not so much rebellion as it is human pride, or hubris, the human desire to be as God.

Reinhold Niebuhr (1892–1971) has presented us with a modern and persuasive interpretation of this ancient story. Coming from a confessional ecclesiastical background, the German Reformed Church, Niebuhr was deeply influenced by his commanding liberal teachers at Yale Divinity School. His concerns with the agenda of the liberals and, particularly, their stress on the exemplary role of Jesus of Nazareth became tested during his time as a pastor of a working-class church in Detroit in the years leading to the Great Depression. His parishioners were employees of Henry Ford and caught up in the drudgery of work in modern industrial life. In a later autobiographical statement, he wrote about his growing uneasiness with liberalism and its assumptions. What is liberalism? "I should say primarily faith in man; faith in his capacity to subdue nature, and faith that the subjection of nature achieves life's final good; faith in man's essential goodness, to be realized either when man ceases to be spiritual and returns to nature (romanticism), or when he ceases to be natural and becomes rational; and finally, faith in human history which is conceived as a movement upward by a force immanent within it."[3]

This liberal optimism could not be responsive to the diabolical element in human civilization that Niebuhr came to see. But neither could "orthodox" Christianity. "The weakness of orthodox Christianity lies in its premature identification of the transcendent will of God with canonical moral codes, many of which are merely primitive social standards, and for development of its myths into a bad science."[4] Niebuhr saw "prophetic" Christianity as the needed voice. Here is how he sought to make the Garden of Eden story meaningful to his time:

> We are deceivers, yet true, when we say that
> man fell into evil. The story of the fall of man
> in the Garden of Eden is a primitive myth which
> modern theology has been glad to disavow, for
> fear that modern culture might regard belief in it
> as a proof of the obscurantism of religion. In
> place of it we have substituted various accounts
> of the origin and the nature of evil in human
> life. Most of these accounts, reduced to their
> essentials, attribute sin to the inertia of nature,
> or the hypertrophy of impulses, or to the defect
> of reason (ignorance), and thereby either explic-
> itly or implicitly place their trust in developed
> reason as the guarantor of goodness. In all of
> these accounts the essential point in the nature of
> human evil is missed, namely, that it arises from
> the very freedom of reason with which man is
> endowed. Sin is not so much a consequence of
> natural impulses, which in animal life do not
> lead to sin, as of the freedom by which man is
> able to throw the harmonies of nature out of
> joint. He disturbs the harmony of nature when
> he centres his life about one particular impulse
> (sex or the possessive impulse, for instance) or
> when he tries to make himself, rather than God,
> the centre of existence. This egoism is sin in its
> quintessential form. It is not a defect of creation
> but a defect which becomes possible because
> man has been endowed with a freedom not
> known in the rest of creation.[5]

When, therefore, one reads the account in Genesis 2 of the Garden of Eden, one must not read it as history. "The idea of the fall is subject to the error of regarding the primitive myth of the garden, the apple and the serpent, as historically true." But the story is not historical. "The fall does not take place in any concrete human act. It is the presupposition of such acts."[6] The image of piety and the image of purity are simply not compatible with that reading of the story. For the Pietist, sin is an action that conceivably could have been avoided; for the fundamentalist, too, sin results from an act of disobedience. Each has a moralistic tone that I believe is incompatible with Niebuhr's reading; his understanding of the human situation is not one that prompts assent from those who view the nature of sin differently, whether they are orthodox or liberal. In perceptive and profound words Niebuhr wrote:

> The Christian analysis of life leads to conclusions which will seem morbidly pessimistic to moderns, still steeped as they are in their evolutionary optimism. The conclusion most abhorrent to the modern mood is that the possibilities of evil grow with the possibilities of good, and that human history is therefore not so much a chronicle of the progressive victory of the good over evil, of cosmos over chaos, as the story of an ever increasing cosmos, creating ever increasing possibilities of chaos.[7]

That is the human predicament. We need think only about nuclear power, genetic engineering, body transplants, cold storage of human embryos—the list increases every day of our lives. Our very progress creates new and grander possibilities for evil.

Does this position offer any way in which Christians can understand themselves in relation to the many revolutions—social, political, economic, and scientific— that surround us? Not in terms of a prescribed Christian agenda. In a short paragraph, however, Niebuhr has outlined a position that offers significant though ambiguous guidelines. In *Moral Man and Immoral Society* he wrote: "The truest visions of religion are illusions which may be partially realized by being resolutely believed. For what religion believes to be true is not wholly true but ought to be true and may become true if its truth is not doubted."[8] Here is my translation; I prefer to substitute "Christian faith" for Niebuhr's "religion." A key vision, expectation, and hope of the Christian faith is the establishment of the kingdom of God on earth, the time when justice and equality will prevail among groups, institutions, and individuals. In one sense, that hope is an illusion because the ultimate transformation of history lies beyond history, not within it. Yet, even though true yet never realizable, that expectation may be advanced by being resolutely believed. Though the promise, the goal, may never be reached, it may be approximated. In that process all human structures— political, economic, social—are only approximations and can never be equated with the will of God. Capitalism, quietism, communism, seeming selfless dedication, are transient and temporary, although in particular historical circumstances each may be useful and necessary.

The promise of Protestantism is to find a way to interpret what has been its core—namely, the meaning of redemption, the notion of the atonement. What we have lost is a sense of community, the fundamentally corporate nature of our common humanity. For many, and most particularly for the disenchanted lovers of the church, the traditional interpretations of the atonement are not responsive to the global needs we can no longer avoid. We are one world, and the task of the Christian is to find a way to express a distinctive way of being in the midst of conflicting paths and loyalties, yet one that does not claim an undeserved universality. Niebuhr's analysis of our collective human predicament and his notion of incarnating the kingdom through laboring in our less-than-ultimate circumstances are genuine resources for a new, communal understanding of Protestant Christianity's identity and mission in contemporary America.

Covenant and the Community

The message of the Hebrew prophets Jeremiah and Second Isaiah, both living in the tumultuous sixth century B.C.E., provide a second resource for a new image of Christianity. Each has a strain of individualism, yet neither can be appreciated apart from his understanding of and relation to the Israelite community. Each has been appropriated by the Christian tradition to describe the coming and role of Jesus as the Messiah, but the prophets were not predictors of the future; they were perceptive judges of the religious import of Israel's social and political situation. For instance, in Jeremiah 31:31-34:

> Behold, the days are coming, says the LORD, when I will make a new covenant with the house of Israel and the house of Judah, not like the covenant which I made with their fathers when I took them by the hand to bring them out of the land of Egypt, my covenant which they broke, though I was their husband, says the LORD. But this is the covenant which I will make with the house of Israel after those days, says the Lord: I will put my law within them, and I will write it upon their hearts; and I will be their God, and they shall be my people. And no longer shall each man teach his neighbor and each his brother, saying, "Know the LORD," for they shall all know me, from the least of them to the greatest, says the Lord; for I will forgive their iniquity, and I will remember their sin no more.

That theme of "New Covenant," central to the Hebrew tradition, has been appropriated by Christians in reference to the coming messiah. Yet the covenant is made with the whole people, the community that acknowledges this God of history. Descriptions of Jeremiah as

108

individualistic miss that essential element, the corporate character of the prophetic understanding of the self.

The painful, moving words of Second Isaiah have also been appropriated by Christians in reference to Jesus Christ. They, too, manifest a corporate dimension. The suffering servant, many biblical scholars believe, refers to the community of Israel; the community itself is personified.[9]

> For he grew up before him like a young plant,
> and like a root out of dry ground; he had no
> form or comeliness that we should look at him,
> and no beauty that we should desire him. He
> was despised and rejected by men; a man of
> sorrows, and acquainted with grief; and as one
> from whom men hide their faces he was
> despised, and we esteemed him not.
>
> Surely he has borne our griefs and carried
> our sorrows; yet we esteemed him stricken,
> smitten by God, and afflicted. But he was
> wounded for our transgressions, he was bruised
> for our iniquities; upon him was the chastise-
> ment that made us whole, and with his stripes
> we are healed.
>
> All we like sheep have gone astray; we have
> turned every one to his own way; and the LORD
> has laid on him the iniquity of us all.
>
> Yet it was the will of the LORD to bruise
> him; he has put him to grief; when he makes
> himself an offering for sin, he shall see his
> offspring, he shall prolong his days; the will of
> the LORD shall prosper in his hand; he shall see
> the fruit of the travail of his soul and be satis-
> fied; by his knowledge shall the righteous one,
> my servant, make many to be accounted righ-
> teous; and he shall bear their iniquities (Isa. 53:2-
> 6; 10-11).

We can also easily forget that in the developing Christian movement the church, the community, came before the New Testament. The early Christians did not have a "new" testament; the canon of the New Testament was not established until the fourth century and then only after conflicts over which letters and which gospels were to be of special authority. Rather, the early Christian movement focused on the figure of Jesus and sought to interpret the good news that God was in Christ *reconciling the world*. The community that sought to interpret the meaning of this reality is what brought the Christian faith alive. We have been excessively preoccupied with an individualistic, private, moralistic, rigid understanding of the gospel. We need to recapture the communal creativity that sought the meaning of redemption and atonement in more than the private and solitary salvation of the individual soul. As Christians, we participate in that process of reconciliation and atonement.

On board the *Arbella* before the Puritans embarked at Salem, John Winthrop wrote his sermon "A Model of Christian Charity." That document has often been used to justify the uniqueness of the United States. "We shall be as a City upon a Hill, the eyes of all people are upon us." But the demands on the community that Winthrop saw are too easily ignored and not as frequently quoted. He wrote:

> For this end, we must be knit together in this
> work as one man; we must be willing to abridge
> ourselves of our superfluities, for the supply of
> others' necessities; we must uphold a familiar
> Commerce together in all meekness, gentleness,
> patience and liberality; we must delight in each
> other, make others' Conditions our own, rejoice
> together, mourn together, labor and suffer
> together, always having before our eyes our
> Commission and Community in the work, our
> Community as members of the same body.[10]

Redemption and the Community

Distinctively American contributions to these themes by Josiah Royce, professor of philosophy at Harvard at the beginning of the twentieth century, are suggestive, persuasive, and a third resource for a new image of Protestant Christianity. Immersed in a Calvinistic heritage, Royce never quite left those roots and continued to struggle to find a way to articulate his understanding of the Christian faith. In *The Problem of Christianity* (1914) he wrote: "Historically speaking, Christianity has never appeared simply as the religion taught by the Master. It has always been an interpretation of the Master and of his religion in the light of some doctrine concerning his mission, and also concerning God, man, and man's salvation—a doctrine which, even in its simplest expressions, has always gone beyond what the Master himself is traditionally reported to have taught while he lived."[11]

Royce was unwilling to enter the realm of christological debate, largely because of the paucity of evidence that the Gospels contain. "Hence I have constantly tried, in these discussions, to avoid hazarding any personal impressions of mine about what actually took place on earth at the moment when the Christian religion originated." We know that there were visions of "the risen Lord," and we possess "that body of sayings and of parables which early tradition attributed to the founder." But Royce's focus is not on the "founder," Jesus, but rather on the community itself, particularly as seen in the epistles of Paul. "I in no wise imagine, and have nowhere suggested, that Paul, in any just sense, was the real founder of Christianity. The Christian community into which Paul entered, and whose life he, as convert, so vastly furthered, this—I have said—this, together with its spirit, is the true founder of Christianity."[12]

Three major themes animate Royce's analysis: the community, the human condition, and the atonement. The human being is under the power of sin. "The individual is powerless to escape from his innate and acquired character, the character of a lost soul, or, in Paul's phrase, of a dead man, who is by inheritance tainted, and is also by his own deeds involved in hopeless guilt." The universal community of believers was, in Royce's view, to be the concrete realization of the kingdom of God as proclaimed by Jesus. "Membership in that community is necessary to the salvation of man,"[13] although this community is not specifically associated with any historical institution. It is through this community, established by the mediator, that atonement is effected.

For Royce, each self becomes a knowing self only in relation to other selves: in family, town, nation, and so on. These social units assume a personal quality, and an individual may find fulfillment in his or her allegiance to that community. That devotion Royce terms loyalty. The Christian community saw in the parables of Jesus the ideal of love, though as the community developed, seen particularly in the letters of Paul, it was necessary to make concrete application of this love ideal. Paul "was a critical influence in determining both the evolution and permanent meaning of Christianity." Yet even for "modern man" it is not always clear how the love ideal is to be applied in concrete situations; no appeal can be made to the "simple" teachings of Jesus. Christianity is not a religion of rules and regulations. Since one cannot know another self fully, it is impossible to know how to apply the ideal of love. Even Jesus looked to the end of the world as the time when the full kingdom will appear. For Paul one's relation to another is determined by one's relation to the body of Christ, the divine community, which has a suprapersonal character. "For Paul the neighbor has now become a being who is primarily the fellow member of the Christian community."[14] Salvation is then seen by Royce in the individual's relation to the Christian community, through one's loyalty to the community and the community's loyalty to the individual. For the self there are two foci: loyalty to God and loyalty to the neighbor and community. One's participation in the community, with its common memories and expectations, affords the context in which one makes concrete to the neighbor one's love for God. The church is the concrete embodiment of the ideal but can never be identified with the ideal, not unlike the classical distinction between the invisible and visible church.

Royce was not a naive moralist; in fact there is much in Royce's understanding of human nature that is similar to the realism of Reinhold Niebuhr. He acknowledges that the individual is a product of social training and caught up in pride and self-assertiveness. Sin means separation from the ideal; that is the human predicament; that is the fact of treason under which the human lives. So the self is not a genuine self except in community. Again, the individual's salvation is not effected simply by joining any community. Salvation occurs only with a special community, based on love and strong enough to transform the individual.

The Kingdom and Christian Community

By assembling elements from Reinhold Niebuhr, the Hebrew prophets, and Josiah Royce, we can glimpse a new image for contemporary Protestant Christian identity in America, that resides not in any lopsided emphasis on piety, purity, or plenty but in the image of Christian community enabled by shared loyalty to Christ to participate in the redemptive process of reconciliation. The notion of corporate atonement can address directly the alienation and estrangement that many today feel from themselves, each other, and even the Christian faith itself.

The notion of the atonement does not arise unless the individual or community is aware of the estrangement that pervades existence—estrangement from oneself and the world. We have already reviewed some traditional ways in which this idea has been interpreted in Christian history. The Anselmic interpretation is unsatisfactory not only because of its feudal character but also

113

because reconciliation of the self to the self and community is not a central element. Anselm was concerned only with reconciliation of God to the human. The so-called moral influence view of Abelard does involve a reorientation of the self. It minimizes, however, the communal dimension from which we cannot escape, for human alienation is not only from the self and God but equally from the shattered bonds we have with the rest of humanity. The soteriological focus, then, needs to be not on satisfaction made to God (Anselm) or simply repentance of the individual (Abelard) but on the relation of the self to corporate life.

The idea of vicarious sacrifice, which is an ingredient in the suffering-servant passage of Second Isaiah, may be interpreted not as the one suffering for the many but also as the many suffering for the one. The Christian community takes on sin, the treason that fractures the bonds that unite us. That is its role. Atonement means at-one-ment, making whole, redeeming. In its function as atoning agent, the Christian community suffers and may be required to give up what it has for the sake of a greater good not reachable without such sacrifice. That certainly does not mean, "Sin for the glory of God," as some have verged on saying. Rather, in the inevitable facts of sin, separation, and estrangement there resides the potential for a greater good than there would have been without sin.[15]

The Christian faith is fundamentally about redemption, which involves more than simply forgiveness of sin. One can be forgiven by another—by God, by a friend or enemy. But redemption is costlier; it involves a new, active relationship between the "traitor," to use Royce's term, and the community. Each is transformed, each is engaged.

White mainline Protestantism is already a minority and will remain so. The gospel, however, is not for numbers, but selves: for blacks whose experience whites do not share, for women whose lives are thwarted by expectations either imposed on them or denied to them,

for Indians whose memories have been erased and em-
balmed, for the dispossessed who are forgotten. Those
who claim allegiance to the Christian community come
to it with differing concerns.

So-called mainline Protestantism, which has been
the focus of this volume, has not always known what
to do with such experiences. To take one example, the
black Christian experience includes the fact that Protestant clergy wrote many of the tracts in defense of
slavery in the nineteenth century. And only in the latter
part of this century have we become painfully aware of
the involvement of the white church in the subjection
of blacks and the black church. To make concrete this
interpretation of the atonement as a communal responsibility, we need to listen to what people in the black
churches, among others, have been saying.

> The black church has not only nurtured black
> people but enabled them to survive brutalities
> that ought not to have been inflicted on any
> community of men. Black Theology is the
> product of black Christian experience and reflec-
> tion. It comes out of the past. It is strong in the
> present. And we believe it is redemptive for the
> future.
>
> This indigenous theological formation of
> faith emerged from the stark need of the frag-
> mented black community to affirm itself as a
> part of the Kingdom of God. White theology
> sustained the American slave system and negated
> the humanity of blacks. This indigenous Black
> Theology, based on the imaginative black expe-
> rience, was the best hope for the survival of
> black people. This is a way of saying that Black
> Theology was already present in the spirituals
> and slave songs and exhortations of slave
> preachers and their descendants.
>
> All theologies arise out of communal expe-
> rience with God. At this moment in time, the

black community seeks to express its theology
in language that speaks to the contemporary
mood of black people.

Black Theology is a theology of black liberation. It seeks to plumb the black condition in
the light of God's revelation in Jesus Christ, so
that the black community can see that the gospel
is commensurate with the achievement of black
humanity. Black Theology is a theology of
"blackness." It is the affirmation of black
humanity that emancipates black people from
white racism, thus providing authentic freedom
for both white and black people. It affirms the
humanity of white people in that it says No to
the encroachment of white oppression.

As black theologians address themselves to
the issues of the black revolution, it is incum-
bent upon them to say that the black
community will not be turned from its course,
but will seek complete fulfillment of the promises of the Gospel. Black people have survived
the terror. We now commit ourselves to the
risks of affirming the dignity of black person-
hood.[16]

Here is testimony to weakness and power, to deprivation
and strength, to a costly global view of our common
salvation without platitudes or painless pap. The white
community cannot share the depth of the black experience, but recognition of white participation in the trag-
edies of black Americans is essential to the redemptive
process. So also the experiences of women, gays and
lesbians, and Native Americans must in part be shared
by those who are not themselves oppressed but who do
claim a loyalty to the Christian community. The kingdom of God is an illusion that, according to Niebuhr
"may be partially realized by being resolutely believed."
Such a truth is a call to sacrifice and to redemption from
the curses we have created and quietly nurtured. The

treasons we have committed and reaffirm by our insensitivity and unwillingness to own them can, if we make them ours, produce a renewed community of church and world that would allow a greater good than we have known. Without it the promise of the "good news" will elude us, no matter how pious and pure and plenteously tolerant we might imagine ourselves to be.

The Christian faith and Christian identity are not as simple as many would have us believe. Issues posed in debates between "liberals" and "fundamentalists" are no longer significant ones. The liberal was trying to recapture and emulate a modernized Jesus, and the liberal "lives" of Jesus paint a picture of a man who could heal the fractured human condition if only the encrustations of the tradition were wiped away. Yet in the end, peeling away the layers of the onion has left liberal Christianity with nothing. Equally inadequate is the fundamentalist attempt to call us to a reborn life, relying on the miraculous way in which the Savior has redeemed us from sin and pointing to the unambiguous way to the Christian life and values. Moreover, traditional christological and other doctrinal debates, historically crucial, are increasingly meaningless religiously; both trinitarianism and unitarianism are basically passé issues.

The Christian faith is grounded in the conviction that God acts in history to bring about human redemption. The world was created good, yet disruption, confusion, and sin have become part of the human story. In the Christian community's attempt to become the gathered people, seeking to make real and concrete the ideals of the one called the Messiah, the redemptive process is lived out, even though all the concrete efforts fall short of the ideal. Establishment of the kingdom of God on earth is, in that sense, an illusion yet not to be forsaken. The church is not the kingdom of God but is made up of sinners who seek to make each wayward path healed by the action of the community to which they belong. Beyond that, this Christian community, within the limits of its own time and place, seeks its role in the redemption of all, the universal community of humankind. This image of the Christian faith is perhaps as elusive as any other. But it does call into question those who argue that faith is only a heartfelt experience of being saved (piety), or right belief (purity), and calls us to question radically the various forms (plenty) that too easily claim the label *Christian*.

Notes

Introduction

1. *Time,* May 22, 1989, 94.

2. *Surveys by the Gallup Organization and Gallup International Research Institute for the Center for Applied Research in the Apostolate and the European Values System Study Group* (Princeton, N.J., 1981).

3. Charles Glock and Rodney Stark, *Religion and Society in Tension* (Chicago: Rand McNally, 1965), 118. The Protestant denominations polled included Congregationalists (United Church of Christ), Methodists, Episcopalians, Disciples of Christ, Presbyterians, American Lutherans, Missouri Synod Lutherans, American Baptists, and Southern Baptists. Glock and Stark also included "sects" as a category, as well as Roman Catholics.

4. For a survey of recent theological themes, see Deane W. Ferm, *Contemporary American Theologies* (New York: Seabury Press, 1981).

CHAPTER 1: Images of Protestantism in America

1. Thomas Jefferson, "An Act for Establishing Religious Freedom" (1779), quoted in *Cornerstones of Religious Freedom in America,* ed. Joseph Blau (New York: Harper Torchbook, 1964), 78.

2. Hector St. John de Crevecoeur, *Sketches of Eighteenth Century America,* ed. Henri Bourdin, Ralph H. Gabriel, and Stanley T. Williams (New Haven: Yale University Press, 1925), 153–54.

3. James Bryce, *The American Commonwealth* (New York: Macmillan, 1910), 769–70.

4. Francis Grund, *The Americans in Their Moral, Social, and Political Relations* (Boston: Marsh, Capen & Lyon, 1837), 164–65.

5. John Leng, *America in 1876 (Pencillings during a Tour in the Centennial Year)* (Dundee: Dundee Advertiser Office, 1877), 293–94.

6. George Lewis, *Impressions of America and the American Churches* (Edinburgh: W. P. Kennedy, 1845), 398–99, 102.

7. Bryce, *The American Commonwealth,* 779.

8. Charles Lyell, *Travels in North America, in the Years 1841–1842,* 2 vols. (New York: Wiley & Putnam, 1845), 1:96–97.

9. Leng, *America in 1876,* 44.

10. Grund, *The Americans,* 164.

11. See chapter 4, below.

12. Grund, *The Americans,* 166.

13. Gilbert Chesterton, *What I Saw in America* (New York: Dodd Mead, 1922), 260–61.

14. *The Works of Robert G. Ingersoll,* 12 vols., ed. Clinton P. Farrell (New York: Dresden Publishing, 1907), 5:176–77. Hereafter in this section, volume and page citations in the text refer to this work.

15. William McLoughlin, "Is There a Third Force in Christendom?" *Daedalus,* Winter 1967, 51.

16. *The New York Times,* June 12, 1989.

17. Jerry Falwell, *Listen, America!* (Garden City, N.Y.: Doubleday, 1980), 56, 65.

18. Ibid., 244, 263.

19. This "Christian Bill of Rights," sponsored by Jerry Falwell and the Old Time Gospel Hour, appeared as an advertisement in national magazines and as a mailing in October 1980. It is also cited in Peggy L. Shriver, *The Bible Vote: Religion and the New Right* (New York: The Pilgrim Press, 1981), 18–19.

CHAPTER 2: The Image of Piety

1. Sydney Ahlstrom, *A Religious History of the American People* (New Haven: Yale University Press, 1972), 236.

2. *The Social Teachings of the Christian Church* (London: Allen & Unwin, 1931).

3. *The Kingdom of God in America* (New York: Harper, 1935).

4. William G. McLoughlin, "Pietism and the American Character," in *The American Experience* (Boston: Houghton Mifflin, 1968), 41–45. McLoughlin, the foremost student of Pietism in America, first wrote this essay in 1964. It is a refreshingly open-ended and unfinished interpretation of broad themes.

5. Augustine, *Four Books against the Pelagians,* quoted in *Readings in the History of Christian Thought,* ed. Robert L. Ferm (New York: Holt, Rinehart & Winston, 1964), 282.

6. Pelagius, "A Letter to Demetrias," quoted in Ferm, *Readings,* 295.

7. John Calvin, *Institutes of the Christian Religion,* trans. John Allen (Philadelphia: Westminster Press, n.d.), 3.21.181.

8. James Arminius, "Declaration of Sentiments," in *The Works of James Arminius* (Buffalo: Derby, Miller & Orton, 1853), vol. 1, quoted in Ferm, *Readings,* 390.

9. John Wesley, "A Letter to John Newton," in *John Wesley,* ed. Albert Outler (New York: Oxford University Press, 1964), 78.

10. See J. L. Peters, *Christian Perfection and American Methodism* (New York: Abingdon, 1956).

11. John Wesley, "The Fullness of Faith," in Outler, *John Wesley,* 267.

12. John Wesley, quoted in Outler, *John Wesley,* 78.

13. Charles Finney, "Sinners Bound to Change Their Own Hearts," in *Sermons on Important Subjects* (New York, 1836), quoted in Robert L. Ferm, *Issues in American Protestantism* (Garden City, N.Y.: Doubleday, Anchor Books, 1969), 165.

14. McLoughlin, "Pietism and the American Character," 39.

15. William Warren Sweet, *Religion on the American Frontier: The Baptists (1783–1830)* (New York: Henry Holt, 1931), 50–51. See also William Warren Sweet, *Religion on the American Frontier: The Methodists* (Chicago: University of Chicago Press, 1946). Both volumes are gold mines of information.

16. Charles Grandison Finney, *Memoirs of Charles G. Finney, Written by Himself* (New York: A. S. Barnes, 1876), 350–51.

17. Asa Mahan, *Scripture Doctrine of Christian Perfection* . . . (Boston: D. S. King, 1840), quoted in H. Shelton Smith, Lefferts Loetscher, and Robert T. Handy, *American Christianity,* 2 vols. (New York: Charles Scribner's Sons, 1963), 2:44.

18. Charles G. Finney, *Reflections on Revival,* comp. Donald W. Dayton (Minneapolis: Bethany Fellowship, 1979), 50–51.

19. Finney, of course, had his critics. One of them, John Williamson Nevin, a Scotch–Irish Presbyterian who became

a leader in the German Reformed Church (a powerful combination, one that would brook no theological laxity), wrote a tract entitled *The Anxious Bench,* in which he argued: "Finneyism is only Taylorism reduced to practice, a low shallow pelagianizing theory of religion runs through it from beginning to end. The fact of sin is acknowledged but not in its true extent" (2d ed. [Chambersburg, Pa., 1844], 114). Nevin put his finger on the issue!

20. See Leroy Froom, *The Prophetic Faith of Our Fathers,* 4 vols. (Washington, D.C.: Review and Herald, 1946–54).

21. Quoted in Clara Endicott Sears, *Days of Delusion* (New York: Houghton Mifflin, 1924), 35–36.

22. See William Shewmaker, "The Training of the Protestant Ministry in the United States of America, before the Establishment of Theological Seminaries," *Papers of the American Society of Church History,* 2d ser., 6 (1921):126. See also Mary L. Gambrell, *Ministerial Training in Eighteenth Century New England* (New York: Columbia University Press, 1937; reprint, New York: AMS Press, 1967).

23. See Robert L. Ferm, "Joseph Bellamy and His 'School for Prophets' in Eighteenth Century New England," *Bulletin of the Congregational Library* 37 (Fall 1985).

24. Text in Sweet, *Religion: The Baptists,* 1851–91.

25. Antoinette Brown was probably the first woman ordained to the Christian ministry, being set apart by the Congregationalists in 1853. The right of women to be ordained was slowly won in the nineteenth century and then only in those denominations of congregational polity where women more frequently assumed an equal role in lay affairs. Women did serve as lay evangelists. Certainly many women shared pietistic, perfectionist, and millennialist themes, including Barbara Heck, called the mother of American Methodism; Phoebe Palmer, evangelist in the Holiness/Perfectionist movement; and Ellen Harmon White, a leader within Seventh-Day Adventism for decades. See Barbara Brown Zikmund, "The Struggle for the Right to Preach," in Rosemary Radford Ruether and Rosemary Skinner Keller, *Women and Religion in America,* vol. 1, *The Nineteenth Century* (San Francisco: Harper & Row, 1981), 193–241; also Martha Tomhave Blauvert, "Women and Revivalism," in ibid., 1–45.

26. William Lawrence, "The Relation of Wealth to Morals," in *Democracy and the Gospel of Wealth,* Gail Kennedy, ed. (Boston: Heath, 1949), 69.

27. Calvin, *Institutes*, 3.21.181.

28. Russell Conwell, *Acres of Diamonds* (New York: Harper, 1915), text in Ferm, *Issues in American Protestantism*, 236–37, 241.

29. John Preston, *A Remedy against Coveteousnesses in Four Godly and Learned Treatises* (London, 1633), quoted in Stephen Foster, *Their Solitary Way: The Puritan Social Ethic in the First Century of Settlement in New England* (New Haven: Yale University Press, 1971), 112. The reference is to Max Weber, *The Protestant Ethic and the Spirit of Capitalism* (New York: Charles Scribner's Sons, 1958).

30. Quoted in Foster, *Their Solitary Way*, 121.

CHAPTER 3: The Image of Purity

1. These core beliefs have been noted by many. See, for example, Francis Schaeffer, *The Great Evangelical Disaster* (Westchester, Ill.: Crossway Books, 1984), 74.

2. *American Religious Heretics*, ed. George H. Shriver, (Nashville: Abingdon, 1966).

3. Schaeffer, *The Great Evangelical Disaster*, 163.

4. Harold Lindsell, *The New Paganism* (San Francisco: Harper & Row, 1987), 217–18.

5. George M. Marsden, *Fundamentalism and American Culture* (New York: Oxford University Press, 1980), 4, 231 n. 4.

6. Shailer Mathews, *The Faith of Modernism* (New York: Macmillan, 1924), 23, 31, 34, 12.

7. Ibid., 48, 52.

8. Shailer Mathews, "Theology as Group Belief," in *Contemporary American Theology: Theological Autobiographies*, ed. Vergilius Ferm, 2d ser. (New York: Round Table Press, 1933), 173.

9. J. Gresham Machen, "Christianity in Conflict," in Ferm, *Contemporary American Theology*, 2 vols. (New York, 1932), 1:270.

10. J. Gresham Machen, *Christianity and Liberalism* (New York: Macmillan, 1923), 2, 7.

11. Ibid., 73–74, 78–79, 108. Machen's suspicions of the liberals were not unfounded, as seen in Harry Emerson Fosdick, the noted Presbyterian turned Baptist preacher. See his *Assurance of Immortality* (New York: Macmillan, 1913).

12. Norman Furniss, *The Fundamentalist Controversy, 1918–1931* (New Haven: Yale University Press, 1954).

13. H. Richard Niebuhr, "Fundamentalism," in *Encyclopedia of the Social Sciences* (New York, 1938), 5:527.

14. C. Allyn Russell, *Voices of American Fundamentalism* (Philadelphia: Westminster Press, 1976).

15. Ernest Sandeen, *The Origins of Fundamentalism* (Philadelphia: Fortress Press, 1968).

16. Ibid., 5–6.

17. Ibid., 13–14.

18. Marsden, *Fundamentalism and American Culture*, 205, 211.

19. Dennis Duling, *Jesus Christ through History* (New York: Harcourt Brace Jovanovich, 1979), 134–35.

20. Peter Gay, *The Enlightenment: An Interpretation* (New York: Alfred Knopf, 1966), 338.

21. Ibid., 406.

22. Lindsell, *The New Paganism*, xiv.

23. See George Marsden, *Reforming Fundamentalism: Fuller Seminary and the New Evangelicalism* (Grand Rapids: Eerdmans, 1987).

24. Lindsell, *The New Paganism*, 45, 81, 84, 87.

25. Ibid., 104–5. A few decades earlier a fundamentalist was quoted as saying, "The Modernist juggles the statements of Christ's deity, making him a Jewish bastard, born out of wedlock and stained forever with the shame of his mother's immorality" (quoted in Furniss, *Fundamentalist Controversy*, 22).

26. Lindsell, *The New Paganism*, 106, 122.

27. Ibid., 127, 129, 132.

28. Ibid., chap. 7, "The New Pagan Zeitgeist," and p. 141. For Lindsell, the evangelical/confessional theology of Karl Barth also shows the effects of Enlightenment thought. Barth holds that there are errors in Scripture and insists that the resurrection of Christ was "real" only for believers and that the atonement was for all. He does not affirm the "sinlessness" of Jesus; he "dehistoricizes" Scripture. He is, therefore, a child of the Enlightenment. In short, Barth's theology is inadequate because there is no affirmation that the Word of God, Scripture, is inerrant (174).

29. Rudolf Bultmann, "New Testament and Mythology," in *Kerygma and Myth: A Theological Debate*, ed. Hans Bartsch (London: SPCK, 1957), 1–3.

CHAPTER 4: The Image of Plenty

1. Apparently this phrase was first used in 1802 by Thomas Jefferson in a letter to the Baptist Association of Danbury, Connecticut.

2. "The Cambridge Platform, 1648," in *The Creeds and Platforms of Congregationalism,* ed. Williston Walker (Philadelphia: Pilgrim Press, 1960; orig. pub., New York: Charles Scribner's, 1893), 221, 236–37.

3. Ola Elizabeth Winslow, *Meetinghouse Hill: 1630–1783* (New York: W. W. Norton, 1972), 51.

4. Perry Miller and Thomas Johnson, *The Puritans,* 2 vols. (New York: Harper Torchbook, 1963), 1:43.

5. Albert E. Bergh, ed., *The Writings of Thomas Jefferson* 20 vols. (Washington, D.C.: Issued under the auspices of The Thomas Jefferson Memorial Association of the United States, 1903–04), 15:383–85; excerpted in H. Shelton Smith, Lefferts Loetscher, and Robert T. Handy, 2 vols. *American Christianity* (New York: Charles Scribner's Sons, 1960), 1:516.

6. *The Autobiography of Benjamin Franklin,* ed. Nathaniel E. Griffin (Chicago: Scott, Foresman, 1907), 134–35.

7. Robert T. Handy, *A Christian America* (New York: Oxford University Press, 1984), 19.

8. Alan Heimert and Perry Miller, *The Great Awakening* (New York: Bobbs Merrill, 1967), lxi.

9. Text in Joseph Blau, ed., *Cornerstones of Religious Freedom in America* (New York: Harper Torchbook, 1964), 84–85.

10. For a careful analysis of these debates, see Michael J. Malpin, *Religion and Politics: The Intentions of the Authors of the First Amendment* (Washington, D.C.: American Enterprise Institute, 1978). For a different interpretation, see Leonard W. Levy, *Original Intent and the Framers' Constitution* (New York: Macmillan, 1988).

11. Malpin, *Religion and Politics,* 14.

12. *Autobiography of Peter Cartwright: The Backwoods Preacher,* ed. W. P. Strickland (New York: Hunt & Eaton, 1856), 206–8.

13. Edwin Gaustad, *Historical Atlas of Religion in America,* 2d ed. (New York: Harper & Row, 1976), 4, 43.

14. The frequently used estimate that at the time of the Revolution one in ten Americans had a particular religious affiliation has recently been questioned. See Patricia Bonomi

and Peter Eisenstadt, "Church Adherence in Eighteenth Century British American Colonies," *William and Mary Quarterly* 39 (1982): 245–86. More clarification on what constituted church membership is needed. Ezra Stiles, then president of Yale, commented that many Americans were "Nothingarians" (ibid., 270).

15. *Everson v. Board of Education,* 330 U.S. 1 (1947).

16. Ibid.

17. *Zorach v. Clauson,* 343 U.S. 306 (1952).

18. This comment is quoted in Henry J. Abraham, *Freedom and the Court* (New York: Oxford University Press, 1977), 293. His source should be *McCollum v. Board of Education,* 333 U.S. 203 (1948).

19. *Wisconsin v. Yoder,* 406 U.S. 205.

20. *Engle v. Vitale,* 370 U.S. 421 (1962).

21. *Lemon v. Kurtzman,* 403 U.S. 602 (1971).

22. William O. Douglas, *The Court Years 1939–1975: The Autobiography of William O. Douglas* (New York: Random House, 1980), 8.

23. Robert Bellah, "Civil Religion in America," *Daedalus: Journal of the American Academy of Arts and Sciences,* 96/1 (Winter 1967), reprinted in Russell Richey and Donald Jones, *American Civil Religion* (New York: Harper & Row, 1974), 33.

24. Conrad Cherry, *God's New Israel: Religious Interpretations of American Destiny* (Englewood Cliffs, N.J.: Prentice-Hall, 1971), 11–12.

25. See Lloyd Warner, *American Life: Dream and Reality* (Chicago: University of Chicago Press, 1953), 1.

26. Will Herberg, *Protestant, Catholic, Jew: An Essay in American Religious Sociology* (Garden City, N.Y.: Doubleday, 1955). See also A. Roy Eckhart, *The Surge of Piety in America* (New York: Association Press, 1958); Martin E. Marty, *The New Shape of American Religion* (New York: Harper & Brothers, 1959).

27. See especially Marcus L. Hansen, *The Problem of the Third Generation Immigrant* (Rock Island, Ill.: Augustana Historical Society, 1938).

28. Will Herberg, "Religion and Culture in Present-Day America," in *Roman Catholicism and the American Way of Life,* ed. Thomas T. McAvoy (Notre Dame, Ind.: University of Notre Dame Press, 1960), cited in Robert L. Ferm, *Issues in American Protestantism* (Garden City, N.Y.: Doubleday, Anchor Books, 1969), 360.

29. Sidney Mead, "The Post Protestant Concept and America's Two Religions," in *The Nation with the Soul of a Church* (New York: Harper & Row, 1975), 19–20, 23. See also Sidney Mead, *The Lively Experiment: The Shaping of Christianity in America* (New York: Harper & Row, 1963), and *The Old Religion in the Brave New World* (Berkeley: University of California Press, 1977).

30. See Robert Wuthnow, *The Restructuring of American Religion* (Princeton, N.J.: Princeton University Press, 1988) and Erling Jorstad, *Holding Fast/Pressing On Religion in America in the 1980s* (New York, N.Y.: Praeger Publishers, 1990).

CHAPTER 5: Re-Imaging Protestantism in America

1. Anselm, *Cur Deus Homo* (La Salle, Ill.: Open Court, 1954).

2. Peter Abelard, *Exposition of the Epistle to the Romans,* in *A Scholastic Miscellany,* trans. Eugene Fairweather (Philadelphia: Westminster Press, 1956), text in *Readings in the History of Christian Thought,* ed. Robert L. Ferm (New York: Holt, Rinehart & Winston, 1964), 243.

3. Reinhold Niebuhr, "Ten Years That Shook My World," *Christian Century,* April 26, 1939, text in Robert L. Ferm, *Issues in American Protestantism* (Garden City, N.Y.: Doubleday, Anchor Books, 1969), 316.

4. Reinhold Niebuhr, *An Interpretation of Christian Ethics* (New York: Image Books, 1956; orig. pub., New York: Harper, 1935), 18.

5. Reinhold Niebuhr, *Beyond Tragedy* (New York: Charles Scribner's Sons, 1955; orig. pub., 1937), 10–11.

6. Ibid., 11.

7. Niebuhr, *An Interpretation of Christian Ethics,* 92.

8. Reinhold Niebuhr, *Moral Man and Immoral Society* (New York: Scribner's, 1960; orig. pub., 1932), 80.

9. A review of the literature can be found in Christopher North, *The Suffering Servant in Deutero-Isaiah: An Historical and Critical Study,* 2d ed. (London: Oxford University Press, 1973), and *The Anchor Bible Second Isaiah,* introduction, translation, and notes by John L. McKenzie (Garden City, N.Y.: Doubleday, 1968).

10. John Winthrop, "A Model of Christian Charity," text in Ferm, *Issues in American Protestantism,* 9–10.

11. Josiah Royce, *The Problem of Christianity* 2 vols. (New York: Macmillan, 1913), 1:25.

12. Ibid., 2:337–38.

13. Ibid., 1:42–43, 39. In a letter Royce wrote: "As for what my present position means, there is here space to say only this:—For me, at present, a genuinely and loyally united community, which lives a coherent life, is, in a perfectly [literal] sense, a person. Such a person, for Paul, the Church of Christ was. On the other hand, any human individual person, in a perfectly literal sense, is a community" (*The Letters of Josiah Royce,* edited and with an introduction by John Clendenning [Chicago: University of Chicago Press, 1970], 646).

14. Royce, *The Problem of Christianity,* 1:78, 97.

15. Royce also discussed this theme. "This triumph over treason can only be accomplished by the community, or on behalf of the community, through some steadfastly loyal servant who acts, so to speak, as the incarnation of the very spirit of the community itself. This faithful and suffering servant of the community may answer and confound treason by a work whose type I shall next venture to describe, in my own way, thus: First, this creative work shall include a deed, or various deeds, for which only just this individual treason shall give the occasion, and supply the condition of the creative deed which I am in ideal describing. Without just that treason, this new deed (so I am supposing) could not have been done at all. And hereupon the new deed, as I suppose, is so ingeniously devised, so concretely practical in the good which it accomplishes, that, when you look upon the human world after the new creative deed has been done in it, you say first, 'This deed was made possible by that treason'; and secondly, '*The world, as transformed by this creative deed, is better than it would have been had all else remained the same, but had that deed of treason not been done at all. . . .*' That is, the new creative deed has made the new world better than it was before the blow of treason fell" (ibid., 306–8).

16. "Statement by the National Committee of Black Churchmen, June 13, 1969," in *Black Theology: A Documentary History, 1966–1979,* ed. Gayraud S. Gilmore and James H. Cone (Maryknoll, N.Y.: Orbis Books, 1979), 100–02.

Bibliography

General

Ahlstrom, Sydney. *A Religious History of the American People.* New Haven: Yale University Press, 1972.

Cherry, Conrad. *God's New Israel: Religious Interpretations of American Destiny.* Englewood Cliffs, N.J.: Prentice-Hall, 1971.

Gaustad, Edwin. *Historical Atlas of Religion in America.* 2d ed. New York: Harper & Row, 1976.

Handy, Robert T. *A Christian America: Protestant Hopes and Historical Realities.* 2d ed. New York: Oxford University Press, 1984.

Hudson, Winthrop. *The Great Tradition of the American Churches.* New York: Harper & Row, 1953.

Mead, Sidney. *The Lively Experiment: The Shaping of Christianity in America.* New York: Harper & Row, 1963.

————. *The Old Religion in the Brave New World: Reflections on the Relation between Christendom and the Republic.* Berkeley: University of California Press, 1977.

Niebuhr, H. Richard. *The Kingdom of God in America.* New York: Harper, 1935.

Ruether, Rosemary Radford, and Rosemary Skinner Keller. *Women and Religion in America.* Vol. 1, *The Nineteenth Century;* vol. 2, *The Colonial and Revolutionary Periods;* vol. 3, *1900–1968.* San Francisco: Harper & Row, 1981–86.

Smith, H. Shelton, Lefferts Loetscher, and Robert T. Handy. *American Christianity: An Historical Interpretation with Representative Documents.* Vol. 1, *1607–1820;* vol. 2, *1820–1960.* New York: Charles Scribner's Sons, 1960–63.

Special Topics

Barr, James. *Fundamentalism.* Philadelphia: Westminster Press, 1977.

Bellah, Robert N. *The Broken Covenant: American Civil Religion in Time of Trial.* New York: Seabury Press, 1975.

Bercovitch, Sacvan. *The American Jeremiad.* Madison: University of Wisconsin Press, 1978.

Doan, Ruth Alden. *The Miller Heresy, Millennialism, and American Culture.* Philadelphia: Temple University Press, 1987.

Edel, William. *Defenders of the Faith: Religion and Politics from the Pilgrim Fathers to Ronald Reagan.* New York: Praeger, 1987.

Ferm, Deane W. *Contemporary American Theologies.* New York: Seabury Press, 1981.

Finney, Charles Grandison. *Lectures on Revivals of Religion.* Edited by William G. McLoughlin. Cambridge: Harvard University Press, 1960.

Fox, Richard W. *Reinhold Niebuhr, 1892–1971.* New York: Pantheon Books, 1985.

Gaustad, Edwin S. *Dissent in American Religion.* Chicago: University of Chicago Press, 1973.

————, ed. *The Rise of Adventism: Religion and Society in Mid Nineteenth Century America.* New York: Harper & Row, 1974.

Gay, Peter. *The Enlightenment: An Interpretation.* New York: Alfred Knopf, 1966.

Hadden, Jeffrey, and Charles E. Swann. *Prime Time Preachers: The Rising Power of Televangelism.* Reading, Mass.: Addison-Wesley, 1981.

Hutchison, William R. *The Modernist Impulse in American Protestantism.* Cambridge: Harvard University Press, 1976.

Jorstad, Erling. *Holding Fast/Pressing On Religion in America in the 1980s.* New York: Praeger Publishers, 1990.

Kelley, Dean M. *Why Conservative Churches Are Growing.* 2d rev. New York: Harper & Row, 1977.

Lincoln, C. Eric, ed. *The Black Experience in Religion: A Book of Readings.* Garden City, N.Y.: Anchor/Doubleday, 1974.

McBrien, Richard P. *Caesar's Coin: Religion and Politics in America.* New York: Macmillan, 1987.

McLoughlin, William G. *Modern Revivalism: Charles Grandison Finney to Billy Graham.* New York: Ronald Press, 1959.

Marsden, George. *Fundamentalism and American Culture.* New York: Oxford University Press, 1980.

Marty, Martin E. *The Infidel: Free Thought and American Religion.* Cleveland, Ohio: Meridian Books, 1961.

———. *Modern American Religion.* Vol. 1, *The Irony of It All.* Chicago: University of Chicago Press, 1986.

———. *A Nation of Behavers.* Chicago: University of Chicago Press, 1976.

Mead, Sidney E. *The Nation with the Soul of a Church.* New York: Harper & Row, 1975.

Miller, William Lee. *The First Liberty: Religion and the American Republic.* New York: Alfred Knopf, 1986.

Moore, R. Laurence. *Religious Outsiders and the Making of Americans.* New York: Oxford University Press, 1986.

Morgan, Edmund S. *The Puritan Family: Religion and Domestic Relations in Seventeenth Century New England.* New York: Harper & Row, 1966.

Neuhaus, Richard, ed. *Unsecular America.* Grand Rapids, Mich.: Eerdmans, 1986.

Niebuhr, H. Richard. *Social Sources of Denominationalism.* New York: Henry Holt, 1929.

Richey, Russell, and Donald Jones, eds. *American Civil Religion.* New York: Harper & Row, 1974.

Roof, Wade Clark, and William McKinney. *American Mainline Religion: Its Changing Shape and Future.* New Brunswick, N.J.: Rutgers University Press, 1987.

Solberg, Winton U. *Redeem the Time: The Puritan Sabbath in Early America.* Cambridge: Harvard University Press, 1977.

Turner, James. *Without God, without Creed: The Origins of Unbelief in America.* Baltimore: Johns Hopkins University Press, 1985.

White, Ronald C., and C. Howard Hopkins. *The Social Gospel: Religion and Reform in Changing America.* Philadelphia: Temple University Press, 1976.

Wilmore, Gayraud S., and James H. Cone, eds. *Black Theology: A Documentary History, 1966–1979.* Maryknoll, N.Y.: Orbis Books, 1979.

Wilson, John F. *Public Religion in American Culture.* Philadelphia: Temple University Press, 1979.

Wilson, John F., and Donald L. Drakeman. *Church and State in American History: The Burden of Religious Pluralism.* 2d ed. Boston: Beacon Press, 1987.

Wuthnow, Robert. *The Restructuring of American Religion.* Princeton, N.J.: Princeton University Press, 1988.

Index